The One Full Year Challenge

The Journey to a Better Life and a
Better World Starts Within You

Brad Hardin

The One Full Year Challenge
© 2017 Brad Hardin

ALL RIGHTS RESERVED.

Cover design and One Full Year logo: Rae Melton

ISBN: 1974474224
ISBN 13: 9781974474226

Library of Congress Control Number: 2017913649
CreateSpace Independent Publishing Platform, North Charleston, SC

Printed in the United States of America

To my wife, family, and friends, who have always motivated me to be a better person.

No

Looking

Back

No

More

Excuses

Your

One Full Year

Begins...

Now.

Name:

_____

Date:

_____

Contents

Welcome

Welcome to One Full Year. This is not a get rich quick book. You won't find any tips on how to make $6,243 in your first week of work. This book will not give you advice on how to get the "girl or boy of your dreams" or any date for that matter. It does not contain weight-loss advice on how to lose ten pounds in thirty days or thirty pounds in ten days. Not even one single home remedy on how to get rid of your wrinkles. Simply put, this is not a book filled with "remedies" offering you false hope. This is a real, honest, and genuine challenge that focuses on encouraging and motivating you to make positive changes in your life. While these changes will make your life better, they will ultimately benefit the people around you, and in turn, make the world a better place.

I won't lie to you though. This is going to be hard. Very hard. If you're not up for sacrificing, fighting, and giving your all, this may not be for you. But I know you can do it. I know you have it in you to take this challenge and push through until your journey is complete.

So what is this journey I speak of? This is One Full Year. This is finding it in yourself to be the person whom God desires you to be by making better choices and positive changes in your life for an entire year. If you read that last sentence and thought, "Oh no, not another religious book telling me how to live my life," or, "I don't even believe in God, so this won't help me," I encourage you to keep reading. This is for *every* person. This is for the introvert, the extrovert, the older, the younger, the shy, the warrior, the depressed, the joyful, the athletic, the nerd, the forgotten, the famous, the Christian, and the atheist. Every one of us can be better.

Everyone loves a challenge, but that challenge may not always come in the form of a sporting event or athletic competition. It may not be to the extremes of climbing Mount Everest or exploring the depths of the Krubera Cave. The challenges we attempt might be much simpler such as seeing who can whistle the loudest, eat the fastest, or quote the most movies. In some form or fashion, it is in our human nature to challenge each other and accept or decline such challenges. So what makes OFY more daring than climbing Mount Everest? It's because there is this yearning in each of us to be, well...*better*. We all have a desire deep within us to make positive changes in our lives. And at some point, we realize we need to make better decisions, but we often give way to our selfish desires or look for any excuse we can to put off those changes.

The easiness of procrastination.

The laziness of complacency.

The fearfulness of failure.

The selfish pride within us.

We've all been there before. Maybe you're currently there now.

Hopefully, the reason you picked up this book in the first place is because you realize that there are so many things you wish you were doing that you're not. There are so many times that you said, "I really need to quit (fill in the blank)," but you were afraid of failing...again. Or there are times that you said, "I really wish I would (fill in the blank)," but decided that would be too difficult so you gave up rather easily or never even started. We even tell ourselves that we have no time! This is one of the biggest lie we tell ourselves! If we stop to think about it, we have more time than we realize, we just put it in the wrong place. It's like dropping money in the well instead of the piggy bank while wishing that we had more. The excuse list goes on and on and on.

This book does not contain specific daily challenges. Even though such books serve a great purpose, this book challenges you to make positive changes that are personal to you! That's what makes this journey so fun and unique. You probably already know the important things you need to change.

There is no better feeling than accomplishing or overcoming challenges that we face. How about that feeling when you got a raise at your job for all that hard work and extra effort? Or the feeling of passing what might have been deemed as "the hardest test you ever took" after hours of studying and preparation?

I can promise you one thing; if you accept and accomplish this challenge, it will be one of the greatest achievements in your life!

The feeling of pursuing and producing positive change over the course of an entire year is nothing short of awesome! It will take dedication and hard work every day for 365 days—or 366 if you're reading this during a leap year. After your full year, if you don't like the outcome, you can forfeit all of your changes. You can throw it all away. You can tell yourself that it just wasn't worth it. But I truly believe it will be. I truly believe it will be far more exciting and wonderful than any trophy or prize you ever received for *anything*...and that's saying a lot coming from a sports fanatic.

So, I hope you're ready for this journey. I'm on my second one, and I promise that there is no better feeling than pursuing positive changes and renewing yourself daily. Together, we *are going to* build a community of positive change by helping and encouraging one another along the way. Spread the word, share the joy, and with your help, millions of people around the world will become a part of this awesome and gratifying journey.

Don't make any more excuses.

Don't let anything hold you back.

Don't worry about what you couldn't do before.

Don't not do.

What's your OFY?

Chapter 1

One Full Year

The concept for One Full Year (OFY) has been on my heart and mind for quite some time, which is both a good and bad thing. The good thing is that I realized there were changes in my life I needed to make. These changes were not your everyday, popular, "everyone's doing it" changes such as losing weight, quitting smoking, or starting a new career.

Now, don't get me wrong, those are some great things to change and might even be what you choose to change on your OFY. But the idea for my journey went much deeper. It was so much more than running up to the sporting-goods store and buying the newest treadmill on December 30 in order to exercise at the start of the New Year. It was so much more than thinking about resolutions because the calendar told me to. It meant something to me, it was personal, and I was fully committed!

I didn't write this book to tell you what to change or how to live your life. I wrote it to encourage you to look inside your heart and examine your life to find areas that you can change to be better. You know what you need to change and that's why you get to choose the things which matter to you the most within areas of your life that you recognize need to be changed for good. I am sure as you read through this book, or even before picking this up, there are things currently on your mind that you wish you did more, less, or not at all.

Let me give you one example:

It could be that there is someone close to you, maybe a family member or a former friend, whom you had a "falling out" with in the past. You haven't spoken to this person in years, but it has been in your heart to reach out to him or her. Reaching out to this person, whether or not the falling out was his or her fault or yours, becomes a part of your One Full Year Journey.

"What if he or she doesn't want to talk to me?"

"It was all her fault; I'm not talking to her until she contacts me!"

And the excuse list goes on.

As you will learn in chapter 6, you can control 100 percent of your actions and 0 percent of other people's actions.

This example is just one positive change in the possibility of thousands upon thousands. Many more examples are listed in chapter 3, but here are a few thoughts to get your mind focused.

Maybe you curse too much. Maybe you shouldn't talk behind your enemies' (or even friends') back. Maybe you spend too much time on social media and not enough time with your family. Maybe you shouldn't text and drive. Maybe you should volunteer more in the community. Maybe you should stop eating out and save up money to spend on a family vacation that your spouse has been wanting. Maybe you should save to pay off debt. Maybe you should give your coworkers praise and compliment them when they do a good job instead of always noticing the negatives. Maybe you should mow your neighbor's yard. Maybe you shouldn't watch so much television. Maybe you should go talk to that kid sitting alone at the lunch-room table. Maybe you have been thinking about fostering or adopting a child. Maybe you should talk to your parents or grandparents more often. Maybe you should...commit to whatever is most important to you for One Full Year and see if your life is more fulfilled and others around you are uplifted by your positive changes.

You may be struggling with finances, addiction, forgiveness (for yourself or others), or something similar that's causing you stress, pain, and suffering. This is the time you make the decision to fight and overcome the things that are hurting you, your family, your friends, and even people whom you may not realize you have an impact on.

The purpose of this journey is to commit an entire year to making positive changes in your life. These changes may be emotional, physical, mental, or spiritual.

So, why an entire year?

There are varying philosophies on how long it takes to change a habit or routine. Some say thirty days; others say three months. It really depends on who you ask. As I attempted to make changes in my life over the past several years, I had moments where I was focused on positive changes for about three to six months at a time but then slipped back into my previous behaviors. *I never fully committed.*

This time I wanted to make my changes permanent, and I wanted to expand on them every year thereafter. It wasn't until I committed for an entire year that I started to see *real* change, and these changes were becoming a part of my life. In other words, as I started my second journey, I didn't have to make much of a conscious effort to continue with changes from my first OFY since I had practiced them for twelve months.

(Remember the words *conscious effort* because they will be repeated a lot in this book and are one of the keys to succeeding in your journey.)

Another reason for choosing to go an entire year is because you may need a mentor or accountability partner. Through my experiences, opening up to someone about your past struggles opens the door for people to share with you about their current struggles, which a lot of times are very similar. As you help each other, that connection and relationship will benefit the most if it is steadfast for an entire year, and hopefully even longer than that.

My first OFY journey was exciting, and I can honestly say that it was the most fulfilling, uplifting, and inspirational year of my life. No, I'm not just saying that because I have to convince you to buy into this journey. I would have never finished this book had I not thought this was worth it. And I promise it's more than worth it. But it's not easy. I wish it was, but I would be lying to you if I didn't stress to you over and over that this journey is hard. It could be said that the greatest things in life come from working hard and putting in a lot of time and effort. That's what this is. It's going to be a challenging year and you will have to dedicate time and effort to complete your journey. This will include sacrificing and giving up some things that get in the way and cause distractions. If you truly want to change for the better and you truly want to change the world for the better, you must learn to let go of things that prevent you from doing so.

OFY provides a truly humbling experience, since no one knows what your challenges are.

Hopefully, people can see and hear your changes. They will notice your actions and hear your positive and uplifting words.

On the other hand, there may be some changes that you set your mind to in which you need help to overcome. Going at some things alone could be more difficult than you thought, and maybe you've tried to change things on your own in the past with little to no success. If this is the case, please find an accountability partner or mentor to help you through your journey. Hopefully you can find a close friend who's having the same struggles. Start your journey together!

If you don't have anyone you can turn to for help, please contact OFY through social media, e-mail, or the old-school way of writing a letter. Don't worry, we have some pigeons on standby ready to pick up and deliver all of your mail! (We don't really have pigeons, but would love to read your letters!)

There are also some things that you might want to change by working together with a group. Maybe you want to bring about change in your local community by having a free cookout in the city park, organizing a clothing or food drive, or volunteering with a local school to tutor kids. In these examples, it would be a great idea to share your thoughts and passions with others and get a group of people involved. This can turn into an awesome OFY journey together with your local community! If you have wanted to do such things, don't let anything get in your way. That doesn't mean you jump into something without a plan though. Definitely plan it out first, but don't let a lack of resources or time get in the way. Find wisdom from others, trust in your plan, and take a little something from chapter 7 with you, and see what happens!

Take a moment now, and using the bottom of this page and the top of the next page, write down all the things that you wish you were doing or would like to stop doing. These changes are the immediate things that come to your mind. More than likely, they have been in your heart to change for quite some time, and maybe you have tried to change them already with no success. Put that behind you and start focusing on what lies ahead.

As a reminder, these changes can be emotional (controlling your temper), physical (exercising or playing tennis twice a week), mental (thinking before you speak), or spiritual (praying intently, purifying yourself). There are many other changes that will fall under more than one category, such as mentoring to an at-risk teen or volunteering at a local homeless shelter. I know you have some fresh on your mind, but if you need any help, you can jump ahead to chapter 3 and check out the list of 107 positive changes.

If the list you made is really long, try to pick out three to five things that are the most important for you to change. In other words, choose changes that have been in your heart to change. The things that you are most passionate about.

Let's say you have five things that *you want to stop doing* (smoking, cursing, losing your temper, getting to work late, and watching too much television), and three things *you want to do* (volunteer in your local community, read a new book with your spouse, and have a family game night each week). It will work best if you cut those eight total changes down to three to five. In other words, you should focus on the most important changes such as quitting smoking, controlling your temper, getting to work earlier, having a family game night each week, and volunteering, *while still striving* to eliminate cursing and cut down on TV. You might wait until the next year to read a new book with your spouse.

Confused yet?

What I'm saying is that your OFY goal is to *completely* eradicate the negatives and fulfill the positives. The more you add to your list, the harder it will be to accomplish. I don't want you to completely neglect important changes, but you have to make a very *conscious* and motivated effort to make these changes permanent and complete your journey. *When* you succeed in your first journey, you can add more changes to your next OFY. The neat thing though, using the example above, is that you may unintentionally cut down on watching TV in order to accomplish your most important changes. It's a win-win situation.

Remember the beginning of this chapter where I told you this project had been on my mind and heart for quite some time? And that was a good and bad thing?

Well, I didn't mention the bad thing.

The bad thing was that I kept putting my changes off. I never fully committed. I thought about it, but decided I had other "important" things to do. The hardest part of your OFY journey will be to commit for an entire year. As the idea of failure, not enough time, and commitment get you discouraged, redirect your thoughts to the positive things you will accomplish on your new journey.

So, maybe you've heard of OFY before ever picking up this book. Or maybe this is the very first time you've realized any of this. Either way, you might be asking one important and reasonable question:

Isn't this the exact same thing as a New Year's Resolution?

You know the one where you pick out a new diet or discipline that lasts about four weeks before retreating back to what was easy and comfortable?

The idea of making resolutions is similar, but OFY is much more than that. First of all, the changes you are making go on a much deeper level and the possibilities of what you can change are endless. Second, your OFY can start anytime. You don't have to wait (and shouldn't wait) until January 1.

According to most research found throughout the Internet, only about 8 percent of people who make New Year's resolutions achieve their goal.

Only 8 percent make it through an entire year of change. Some say that low of a number is due to a lack of willpower and self-determination. While that is true, I also believe it's because we choose to change what everybody else is changing. For example, almost every year the top New Year resolutions are losing weight, eating healthy, saving money, and traveling. Those are great things to change, but are you choosing those resolutions because that's the resolution standard? Or do you really believe that's what you need to change? What about meditating once a week, doing the yard work for an elderly neighbor, or being patient with your children or spouse? There are many, many more positive changes that we often think about throughout the year on any given day, but never commit to changing. During your OFY, you can and will choose the most important things that are personal to you. Not because it's the standard resolution and not because the calendar told you it's time to change. *We should be focused on positive changes any time of the year!*

A good friend of mine told me that he and some other friends came up with the idea of starting a weight-loss challenge together. The idea came up right before Thanksgiving, so one person in the group said they should wait until the New Year after the holidays are over before they start their weight-loss challenge. My friend said he looked at the group and said, "No, we're starting right now!"

That's the attitude and drive that you need for this journey. You can start your OFY at any time. Start in April. Start in October. Start on Flag Day.

Don't wait until the New Year. Don't wait one month. Don't wait even one day. You know what you need to change. Do it now!

So, is there anything good about New Year resolutions? Absolutely. The good thing about New Year resolutions is that at this time of year, we start thinking about positive changes. We are eager to start a fresh new year. And, if you are reading this at the start of the New Year, that's fantastic! I don't want you to think that I'm belittling your changes because it's at the beginning of the New Year. That's absolutely not my intention. I just want you to know that there are many positive possibilities, and I want to encourage you to make a real commitment and a real connection to your personal changes.

One Full Year is *not* a New Year's Resolution; it's a *way of life*!

Chapter 2

This Is Not the Challenge the World or Society Offers

Before we dive into this chapter, let me explain to you the meaning of "the world" as it pertains to this chapter. "The world" refers to people who you may or may not know who care absolutely nothing about your well-being. Furthermore, it refers to anyone who is looking to profit from you at the expense of your embarrassment, depression, or hard work. There are a lot of people who claim to be your friend or they claim to care about you, but their only intention is to gain something for their own benefit, not caring if they hurt you in the process. For that reason, I am referring to these people as the "world." I am sure that you know people who are like this, and maybe that person is even you (and that's part of what you're going to change during your OFY journey).

Society, as used in this chapter, will refer to the constant pressure from media, advertisements, and the latest technology to consume and *be consumed* of materialistic goods that come between our meaningful, honest relationships with each other.

In other words, our society is filled with consumption instead of compassion. Society tells you to pursue the "American Dream." The dream of getting to the top, winning the lottery, and obtaining as much property and goods as possible. But that journey is usually filled with heartache and despair, even if you do somehow reach the "American summit."

True happiness is hard to find in the pursuit of "things." More on this thought in a later chapter.

In this chapter, I have divided groups of people into three sections to explain how the world and society play a specific role in discouraging and disparaging you from making good decisions that lead to positive change.

You can read through and choose which section you fall under. You may see things from each section that could apply to you, or you may even decide that none of these sections relate to you at all. If the latter part is true, think seriously about how the world and society can have a positive or negative effect on your OFY journey.

For the Teens

I guess I could say that this part of the chapter is written for all the millennials, but it's hard for me to use that word because, according to most definitions, I fall into this category based on age. However, I don't classify myself, or most of my friends for that matter, as a millennial. So we are going to call this group the "Smartphone and Social Media" group or SPASM for short.

First, let's get one thing clear: it's not your fault that you were born during the SPASM era.

It's not your fault there are tons of advertisements to try to persuade you into buying and consuming products. It's very easy to be consumed with what society has to offer when you're growing up right in the middle of it, especially when it's all around you.

It seems that there are certain expectations that you're supposed to live up to...or maybe that's how you feel. You feel compelled to follow and keep up with everyone on social media. You have immediate access to celebrity news, pop culture, the latest trends and fashions, and all the newest gadgets. This constant pressure to *keep up* with society creates an illusion that might make you feel worthless, lost, and even lead to depression.

Don't let society sell you depression.

Disconnect and reconnect.

In other words, give technology a break and make real, face-to-face connections with your peers, your parents/guardians, and even the elderly. Those relationships will bring about true joy and happiness, much more than the consumption of technology.

As much as there is to say about the subject of social media, I have decided to save it until the end of this chapter, as I believe it directly affects all of us, no matter the age.

But before we get there, let's look at some of the challenges that the world offers a teenager.

Beneficial Challenges?

There are a lot of other challenges that will be presented to you throughout your life, especially at a young age. Some of those challenges bring about good. Some challenges embarrass and humiliate you for others' enjoyment. Some can cause physical harm or even be fatal.

Challenges that bring about good, for example, are when someone tells you that you will never finish or even go to college. You then make it your mission and goal to prove them wrong and walk across the stage to receive your diploma. Someone else might tell you that you will never be good enough to play a particular sport, so you spend countless hours practicing in order to make the team of the sport that you love. Both of these challenges bring about good, positive decisions.

On the other hand, there are a lot of challenges offered to you that have no benefit or intrinsic value and can bring about bad outcomes.

For example, when your friend dares you to take the "Cinnamon Challenge," you gain absolutely nothing from giving it a try. In fact, this particular stunt (which requires you to eat a spoonful of cinnamon within sixty seconds without drinking anything) is very dangerous. The cinnamon can easily restrict the trachea/windpipe, which can cause gagging and lead to choking. Once again, there is no benefit to partaking in this challenge, but I suppose the main purpose of this challenge is so that others can get a good laugh watching you struggle.

That challenge doesn't make you cool.

It doesn't make you look good.

It doesn't make you better.

It basically creates "enjoyment" for others at your own expense.

There are many other examples of "worldly" challenges that do us no good. Seeing how many people you can have sex with, drinking the most alcohol, driving the fastest down an unmarked road or any road for that matter, talking bad about your peers, bullying, and so on.

Somehow society and the world have persuaded you to believe that doing such things makes you "popular." However, society doesn't tell you about the pain and sorrow that you or your peers around you feel after participating in these actions.

Now, I will be the first to admit that I was not immune to taking such challenges when I was younger. There are definitely some challenges that my friends, and so-called friends, dared me to do that I gladly and somewhat reluctantly accepted. So I'm not saying it's easy to avoid everything, nor is it even wrong to accept a few challenges of no benefit.

What I am saying is that we love to take on challenges that have no positive benefit in order to be noticed and accepted by our peers. Isn't it time you accepted a challenge to *better* yourself and ultimately *better* your peers?

Isn't it time to create a new path that your peers will follow to develop better and more positive relationships?

Isn't it time to break societal norms to produce positive change?

What would happen if we shape society instead of society shaping us?

The Initiation Fee

How many times have you chosen to do something just to be accepted or to "fit in" with those around you? How many times have you thought, "I really *don't* want to do this, but I don't want them to think less of me, so I have to?" Or, on the reverse side of that, you felt in your heart you should do the right thing, but you were too worried of what your peers would say about you?

What does it cost to fit in?

I recently had the opportunity to share OFY with a group of teens. I asked if they knew of anyone in their school who didn't have any friends and was bullied by their peers. I received an emphatic "yes" from several teens. I then asked them how come they never talked to or reached out to that person. There was silence for a few seconds until one honest, young girl raised her hand and said she was afraid to talk to that person for fear of what her friends would think of her. For fear that they would walk in the opposite direction when she spoke to the bullied, outcast teen. I first told her that I appreciated her honesty. I then told her that compassion is contagious and hopefully her friends would follow suit if they truly loved her friendship and truly loved *everyone else.*

This seems to be a lifelong theme for teens. Not making choices or making choices only because of what your "friends" will think of you. I think it's called peer pressure. I've been there. We all have at some point.

Young people, and even the "older," let's be the generation that changes that, or at the very least, let's make good decisions that cross our mind first without letting the worry of how others perceive us prevent us from making a positive impact.

And let's be honest. If you reach out to the kid who is lonely and show him or her compassion, and your friends leave you, were they truly your friends to begin with? Or did they hang out with you because you wear the latest popular brand of clothing? Or because you play sports or have the nicest car? If you tell someone no, and they reject you or make fun of you, do you *really* want to be that person's friend? The *cool* thing about OFY is that once you accept this challenge, everything and everyone around you benefits. Your peers see a positive change in you. Your family sees a positive change in you.

They realize there is something different about you. Something good.

Something that's contagious.

You see, while challenges such as the "cinnamon challenge" might get you a few "bonus points" on the "cool" scale, they don't make you a better person, or the world a better place.

Start Side Note

Not everything you choose to change has to be about your character or personality. Remember, these changes can be spiritual, physical, or emotional.

For example, you may have been eyeballing a car for the last year or so, but you have done nothing to obtain it because you just think there is no way you can afford it (or maybe you're expecting your parents to buy it). After all, you've got friends to hang out with, sports to play, tests to study for, and so many other things that get in the way. You have no time...or do you? What if you spent OFY working various jobs and saving every last penny possible? What would happen? You might just save up enough money to buy the car, or maybe your parents will help after they've seen your hard work. This is just one example. There are many other things that we want to do, but we just don't. In Chapter 3, I have listed 107 different things you can do on your OFY journey. But that's only the beginning. That list is only ideas. You make the choice. You make the commitment. You make the change.

You see, the problem is that we long to have, but we don't want to put in the effort to obtain. We want nice things immediately and a lot of times we want them given to us. However, if we work really hard, we can accomplish, and that feeling of accomplishment is like no other.

End Side Note

I've got a confession.

When I was younger (in my teens and early twenties), the world revolved around me.

Can you imagine that?

The world was orbiting around a self-centered core deep within me. My thoughts were for my personal gain. My actions were mostly for my benefit, and mostly to make me "popular." Every now and then I did something good to help others, but I didn't make a habit of it.

One of the hardest things about being a young person is that a lot of our decisions are based on how others will perceive us. After all, we want to be accepted by our peers.

My first sip of alcohol was at a high-school party. I drank that night because everyone around me had, and I *thought* I had to fit in. I even faked being drunk even though I had only taken a few sips because I thought doing so would get me some more "popularity points." I can tell you after that fact that I didn't gain popularity nor did I gain any true friends.

The interesting thing about that night though is that I didn't want to drink.

Wait, what? A teenager not wanting to drink?

That's right. And it wasn't out of fear of getting into trouble with my parents, nor was it because I was a "chicken." I just didn't want to drink alcohol.

And that's perfectly okay. It's okay to say no to things you don't want to do. It doesn't make you less of a person. As a matter of fact, it makes you stronger.

Much...more...stronger.

It makes you stronger because you are making personal choices that you believe are right no matter what someone else pressures you into thinking. The first time you stay strong on what you believe is right, the easier it is the next time and the time after that.

Now, I didn't use this example about alcohol to parent you and tell you what's right and wrong. I brought it up to explain that there are many, many things that you don't want to do, yet do. And, comparably, there are many things you know you should do, but don't.

Remember the list from earlier?

Talking bad about a peer, having sex, bullying, cheating, driving fast, lying, stealing, not talking to another teen, or making fun of someone because he or she looks and acts different, and so on.

Do you partake in these things because that's the "cool" thing, and you feel pressured into doing so?

What if you could change that?

What if you made the decision that crossed your mind first?

What if you made choices that put others ahead of yourself?

You have the unique ability at your age to influence others in a positive way and cause a domino effect of goodness and positive change! You are a very strong and courageous person! Use those qualities to change for the better and change the world!

Remember this, the most unpopular things you do in life make you the most popular. In other words, doing what is good and positive makes you and those around you better.

Young person, don't wait to be better. Don't let your peers pressure you into making poor decisions. Make better decisions and take a step out of your "comfort zone." Those positive decisions will likely have a bigger and more meaningful impact on your peers than you ever could have imagined.

You can make positive decisions no matter what society tries to sell you or tell you. Don't be afraid to do what's right. Don't be afraid to make the harder choices that will ultimately lift up someone through their struggles. This is your chance to make "unpopular" choices and be the positive change the world needs to see!

For the Young (At Heart)

When I divided this chapter into three different sections, I didn't have a particular age limit in mind per group. I figured that as you read through the chapter, you could decide which category you fall under. It may be one or the other, or it may be all three.

The world seems to look at the "older" generation as "out of touch" with modern times. The world often overlooks those who are "beyond their years" because they have little to nothing to offer.

Both of these ideas are completely untrue.

It could be that you're at a point in your life where you feel that you can no longer change anything. Maybe you believe you are "stuck in your ways."

Don't believe this!

You can *always* be better and positively influence people no matter what age you are.

I work in a hospital, and my clientele are mostly from the ages of 50–150. A lot of my inspiration for writing this book and sharing OFY with everyone comes from the wonderful people within this age group.

As an occupational therapist in the hospital, I have literally worked with patients who are on their last breath. I have worked with those who are suffering from cancer, heart failure, and a number of other life-threatening illnesses. Despite all the pain and suffering, I have never seen such upbeat and hardworking individuals in my entire life. I have watched people use every bit of strength they had left to get out of bed, walk ten feet, or even feed themselves.

At the time of writing this book, I had been working with a lady who recently lost her husband after several years of marriage.

She was depressed.

She was hurting.

And she was very sick.

She stayed in the intensive care unit for a few days and it was all we could do to help her sit up on the edge of the bed. For the first few days, her motivation level was poor, and she refused therapy.

It seemed as though she was giving up. The therapy team kept trying to encourage her every day, but she was refusing (and understandably knowing everything she had been through).

She finally agreed and through many tears, she was able to get out of bed and take a few steps. During one of my visits, I told her to stand up with me and we were going to dance. (For the record, I cannot dance.) She used all of her strength to stand up with me for just a few minutes. Before she sat down, she laid her head on my shoulder and started to cry heavily.

As we sat down, I put my arm around her and asked her if I could do anything. She then proceeded to talk about her husband and reminisce on some of their times together. She managed a chuckle as she was thinking about her husband's charm and sense of humor. She thoroughly missed him, but she still fought past the pain and sorrow to better her own health. Her son was there every day at her bedside encouraging and loving her. I think it was through her son that she was able to find the courage and strength to improve her health enough to finally be able to go home.

The great thing about her and so many other people I see on a daily basis is that they work through so much pain and suffering to accomplish their goals. As I worked with several amputees, stroke patients, and so on, I had to ask myself,

What is my excuse?

Did I really have one?

The same thoughts flow through my mind when thinking about the children at St. Jude Children's Research Hospital. I had the wonderful privilege of volunteering for these children and their parents a few years ago. Though most are battling life-threatening diseases, their smiling faces and unshakeable strength is beyond courageous. It's humbling.

Somehow these patients, their families, and many others throughout the hospital and rehab universe find ways to fight. They don't worry about their current state of health. At least that's not their focus. Their focus is on what they can do to better themselves and make the lives of people around them better as well.

That's the whole idea behind OFY. You can absolutely better yourself. It doesn't matter if you're 12 or 112. It doesn't matter if you're working or retired. It doesn't matter if you *think* you're unable because there is someone who has already proven that it's possible.

In preparation for writing this book, I tried to pay more attention to what people were saying. I focused more on their thoughts and emotions on various topics. I have found that this generation of people have mostly become bitter and somewhat distant from the millennials, aka the SPASM group.

Not every young-at-heart is this way, but a vast majority.

I heard people mention several times of how lazy and naïve the younger generation has become. How the popularity of the smartphone and social media has caused young people to be disconnected, withdrawn, unsympathetic, and just plain lazy. While some of this may indeed be the case, it isn't the healthiest approach to reaching out to the millennials. It doesn't do any good to constantly bicker about the bad habits of the younger generation without offering any passionate and humble guidance.

Young-at-heart, the younger folks need your advice, your wisdom, and your love. Instead of grumbling about how things were done "back in my day," how about teaching and sharing wisdom out of love and selflessness?

There are many things that someone younger is currently struggling with that you have been through and overcome.

Help the person.

Give him or her your invaluable knowledge and shed some light on your past experiences.

As a man in my thirties, I crave emotional and spiritual wisdom from those who are older. It does so much more for me than someone telling me how wrong or lazy I am.

Now, I didn't write this section to give a scolding to my elders. I know my grandparents probably wouldn't appreciate that!

I am, however, reaching out to you to explain how important you are and the many things you have to offer! Maybe it has been in your heart to mentor or foster a child.

Don't think twice about it!

Do it!

You could have such a wonderful and beautiful influence on that child. Maybe you have resources or tools that could help a younger person graduate high school, go to college, or get a job. Give freely! There are many teens who would benefit a great deal from your willingness to help!

Remember this: You are *never* too old to learn a new skill or try something for the first time. If you want to learn a new language, go for it! If you want to learn how to swim, jump in! If you want to ride a roller coaster, check with your doctor first! That last one was for laughs. Seriously though, don't let your age be a factor in stopping you from pursuing positive changes and goals. Find a companion to help you and find a way to get it done!

Always keep in mind that you can constantly be finding ways to be better and help others make positive changes, no matter how young at heart you are!

There are no limitations as to how much of a
positive impact you can have on people.

Compassion and courage are not defined by age.

They are defined by you.

Everyone Else in Between

A lot of people who fall into this group may
be raising families, starting careers, searching for
love, searching for purpose, or a combination of
more than one. I can't tell you what career to choose,
who to love, or how to raise your family. I can tell
you, however, that you do have a purpose. If nothing
else in life, you have a purpose to serve others and
make a positive difference in the lives of people
around you. No matter where you come from, what
you look like, how much money you have, or how
smart you think you are, you can bring about great
change to the world in which you currently live in.

Examine where you are right now in your
life.

Are you happy with your job?

Are you happy with your daily routine?

Are you happy with your lifestyle?

You might answer yes to all of these questions and that's a good thing. If you answered no, then make some positive changes on your journey that can bring about happiness in your life. If your family can afford it, switch careers to something you have longed to do. Go back to college and finish your degree or increase your knowledge by obtaining a degree higher than the one you already have. Find ways to strengthen your marriage. Spend more quality time with your children.

Be a Parent

I have only been a parent for a little more than a year, so I'm not going to act like I have all the answers to parenting. I will encourage you, though, to be more of a parent and less of a friend. What does that mean?

Society tries to influence us on how to parent. There is a lot of debate currently on what type of punishment to use on your child and whether or not you should even punish the child at all. I'm not going to suggest one way or the other, but I will give you my honest opinion based on my life experiences and what I have noticed with different parents.

Some parents will give in and give a child exactly what he or she wants when he or she throws a fit. I have even witnessed parents giving a very young child a smartphone to stop them from crying. First of all, if you give a child what they want every time, what will they expect when they are older and out on their own? Better yet, how will they react when they get rejected for a job or want the latest and greatest smartphone, but can't afford it? Will they continue to search for another job? Will they be fine with using a flip phone?

Second, is a smartphone or tablet the answer? I understand that some smartphones have movies or songs that help to calm a child, but ask yourself this question:

Are you giving your phone to your child because that's the only way he or she will calm down, or are you giving your child the phone because you don't want to take the time to *spend a moment with them* to help calm them down?

It's okay to be a friend, but children need a parent. My parents were a little on the strict side when I was growing up. When I was in my teenage years, I noticed a lot of my peers were getting to do just about whatever they wanted. At the time, I was very angry with my parents for "holding me back" from enjoying life. While I didn't understand at the time, I am thankful now.

I realized that they cared.

They weren't trying to keep me from every "bad thing" in life, but they were teaching me to be a part of things that would benefit me in the future. In other words, they were teaching me that my choices *now* would have a negative or positive impact on me *later* in life. Yes, I still made mistakes, and I still got into trouble. But I was aware of where the path led me if I continued making bad choices.

If you are a parent and realize that you could teach a little bit more with love and patience, make that a part of your OFY journey.

Live, love, and laugh with your children, but don't forget to be a parent along the way. Teach them how to be kind, how to serve, and how to show compassion. Teach a better now to create a better tomorrow.

If your smartphone, tablet, or other electronic device gets in the way of doing any of the above, make a commitment on your OFY journey to spend more time with your children. They will be all grown up before you know it, and you never know when you might not have another moment to spend with them.

Single and Serving

Single? No family? Do what your heart is telling you to do. If you're currently searching for a relationship, for someone to spend your life with, work on bettering yourself and serving others first.

That special someone will hopefully be doing the exact same thing and you might end up bumping into each other along the way.

Next, ask yourself this: How are you serving people?

In other words, what is your attitude when you serve? Are you serving to be served? To be seen? To receive a pat on the back?

The most difficult thing about serving is to serve without getting anything back in return. No recognition, no reward, not even a "thank you." There's nothing wrong with receiving these things, but we should be able to serve without even thinking about the reward. I'll be the first to admit it—it's easier to serve when we are appreciated for doing so. When people acknowledge our efforts, we are more likely to continue in our service to others.

However, it's time to change our attitude about service. Try to serve others in such a way that people see the real, genuine love of Christ in you. This requires complete selflessness, sacrifice, and vulnerability. All characteristics of which you possess, but you have to push through the selfishness, pride, and comfortableness that might be stuck in the forefront of your mind.

For everyone between the teens and the young-at-heart, keep this in mind:

Teach and be a positive influence to a child.

Care for the elderly.

Find a job you love or love the job you have.

Put your family above yourself.

Cherish your time with friends and family.

Be a servant to others.

Follow the changes you have in your heart.

All Together Now

Technology has overtaken the world. In many ways, that's a good thing. We have been able to use this vast array of technology to save lives, communicate with each other, create new job opportunities, and so on and so forth. On the other hand, technology can consume us. It can take away our time, our meaningful relationships, and our work ethic. However, it is possible *to choose not* to be consumed by it. Am I saying that you need to give up your smartphone and delete all of your social-media accounts? No...yes...well, actually a combination of both. Puzzled? Keep reading.

Our phones and social media can be great tools to connect with each other. They are also great tools in sharing information and ideas. As a matter of fact, you can find information about OFY on most social-media sites. These resources definitely have their upside, but people can also abuse them and use them in harmful and negative ways.

Three of the biggest problems I have noticed with our use of social media is the war of words between people, the self-indulgence of "self," and the amount of time spent staring at a screen. Teens, adults, and even older adults do this too, so keep reading if you need to be challenged to turn some of these problems into positives.

Problem #1: The Online War of Words

While writing this book, I spent some time reading posts and comments that people made in response to a video, article, or a post from another person. I never knew so much hatred existed in our human population. There was constant bickering back and forth, cussing out each other, calling people hateful names, and even threats on people's lives. And to think that people were doing all of this from behind a computer or phone screen!

Let's get one thing straight—*it's okay to disagree with people*, but at what point do you realize that hurtful words are not doing anybody any good? People are spending several minutes to hours of wasted time being hateful to people they don't even know and have never even seen! I don't know if you have been a victim or suspect to this happening, but it's got to stop. I hope you can find it in your heart to change this during your OFY. Don't respond if you're being negative and don't follow people who are mostly posting negative thoughts on Twitter or Facebook.

It seems like every week there is a new article in the media about two celebrities getting into a "fight" on social media.

Why is this even news?

There are kids battling cancer, families struggling to find their next meal, homeless people trying to find warmth for the winter, and we're worried about millionaires fighting on social media?!

Back to my question from earlier: Should you delete all social-media accounts?

Here's the simple answer: If you can't stop from being negative, then yes, eliminate all social-media accounts.

I know this comes as a shocker since giving that up would basically mean cutting off your dominant hand. But if that's what it comes down to, then do it! Keep in mind that you are making positive changes at whatever the cost, and if that means shutting down social media, even if it's just for a short time, then don't let anything or anybody stop you. If your friends start asking you why you got off social media, you can kindly tell them it's because you needed a break to refocus your thoughts and mind on positive things. Maybe they will even follow your lead.

Problem #2: The Self-Indulgence of *Self*

Kind of sounds redundant, doesn't it? That's because selfishness is redundant. Once you focus your thoughts on yourself, everything you do is about you.

This seems to be a running theme with social media and society in general. Almost everything offered through social media is about *you* instead of your *neighbor.*

Follow closely: You can get an *i*phone and use it to put a video on *You*Tube or post a photo of a *self*ie on *Face*book. It's all about you.

We get so caught up in thinking about ourselves that we forget the people around us who are in need of true companionship. We forget about the people in need of true compassion and true friendship.

There was a great story floating around the Internet and featured on *The Steve Harvey Show* around the summer of 2016.

Four teens witnessed a bad wreck involving a mother and her two kids. The teens rushed to help the mother and calm her children during the aftermath of the accident. They even noticed that she had bought groceries and they had spilled in the back of her trunk, so they offered her some money. After the mother refused to take it, they wrote her a note, slipped the money inside it, handed it to her, and left.

On *The Steve Harvey Show*, the mother said the teens could have used their smartphones to take photos of the wreck and post it on social media or send it to their friends. Instead, they immediately ran to help.

What would you have done in this situation? Would you have whipped out your phone and taken pictures or immediately run to help? How often do you see violence, a car accident, and other instances of people getting injured, sometimes seriously, and whip out your phone to get a picture or video without actually offering help?! Hopefully, we can learn to help first and forget about trying to create the next "viral" video.

While I did mention earlier that social media can be used in a very positive manner, there's not much good to say about selfies.

I'm not talking about the ones with you and your friends or family on vacation or just having a great time being with each other. I'm talking about the selfie of just yourself. The one where you spend countless hours pointing the camera toward yourself in nine hundred different poses. If you have your camera pointed toward yourself, how can you see what's going on around you? Turn the camera around and capture a happy moment of someone else. Or try putting your phone away and experiencing a happy moment with someone else through your own eyes.

Maybe you don't see selfies as a big problem and think they're harmless. You have every right to that opinion. Just ask yourself one question. What is the main reason you're taking a selfie? Is it because you're focused on other people, or is it because you're focused on yourself?

Continuing with the idea of self, how much of your social media is about yourself? Do you use social media to display photos of your accomplishments and consumption of materialistic goods?

There's nothing wrong with showing off your interests, fun times with friends, your family adventures, and so on. But how much of it is bragging about yourself, saying "Look at me," or "Look at what I have?"

How much of it is shining a light on others?

In the same regard, what are your status updates mostly about? Do your status updates constantly bash someone else? Are you once again trying to bring others down and be hateful?

What if you used your status updates to say something positive about someone other than you?

You know all of those negative things you're posting about that are making you unhappy and frustrated. For one entire week (don't worry, you're not getting off that easy), try posting something positive that you see in the news, at work, or in the community. After one week of doing that, assess how that made you feel. Then, continue doing that for an entire year. (You knew it was coming.)

Same goes for reading negative things that frustrate you. Delete the person posting those thoughts or delete your account if you have to. Just don't let that stuff get to you and bring you down. You especially don't need those negative thoughts floating around in your mind during your OFY.

Problem #3: Time spent staring at a screen

While I can't speak for every person in this category, I can give you my honest observation of the majority of people I come in contact with daily. Most people are *engrossed* in their smartphones. I have encountered several people texting or scrolling through their phone with no idea of where they're going. (Yes, I have been guilty of this too.)

Social media and texting have become the center of conversation. So much so that we have lost the ability to have real, connected, face-to-face conversations with each other.

Here are some shocking, or maybe not shocking, statistics found through some credible sources. According to a research study on teens and social media done in 2015 by Pew Research Center, they found that 92 percent of teens who have a mobile phone access the Internet every day.[1]

That's right.

Almost 100 percent of teens are on the Internet through their smartphone every day.

Even worse, about a quarter of these teens report being online "almost constantly."[1]

I think it's safe to say that adults are probably close to the same percentages as teens.

Does this describe you? Do you think it's possible to limit your technology usage?

Take a moment to be honest with yourself and write down how much time you think you spend on your phone or social media per day.

Underneath that, write down three reasons why you spend time on your phone or social media.

Finally, write a yes or no beside each reason if you could do that without using a phone or computer. For example, if one of your reasons you spend time on social media is to talk to friends, write "yes" if you could do that without a device, or "no" if you couldn't.

Remember, be *honest* with yourself.

Time Spent Daily on Smartphone and Social Media:

———————————

Top Three Reasons: 1)

2)

3)

I cannot tell you what changes you need to make during your OFY, but I will offer these challenges to you:

Limit your time on your smartphone and social media. Make real connections and build meaningful relationships with people through face-to-face conversations and real-life interactions. Encourage each other. Stop bullying or help people who are being bullied. Talk with someone who sits alone at lunch or is classified as an "outcast." Break out of your "cliques" and make friends with people who are different from you.

Be the change the world needs to see. Remember the purpose of OFY? It's a yearlong challenge to make positive changes to benefit you and those around you. It is not easy but well worth it!

No matter what age you are.

No matter where you live.

No matter your race.

It's time to join together to break free of our societal norms and develop real, meaningful relationships with each other from ages 13 to 113.

It's time to work together to support each other in making positive changes for ourselves and our communities.

Together, we will build a community of change through our strength, sacrifice, and service to others.

Together, with everyone else making positive changes in their lives, we can, if only for a moment, make the world a better place.

Chapter 3

The Possibilities of Positivity

We like to win. Whether it is a sporting event or an argument, we want to come out on top. Sometimes we will do whatever it takes to win. This can lead us to take extreme measures going so far as to physically and emotionally hurt the other person. And it seems that our culture thrives off hurting others to get what we want.

To emphasize this, I went to YouTube and did a video search on "fight" compared to "sportsmanship." The search for "fight" yielded 76.4 million results, while the search for "sportsmanship" only produced 164,000 results.

Now, I get that sportsmanship is not a very common word and that the word "fight" is a very broad term that can have some positive meanings such as "fighting against cancer," so I decided to change it a bit.

I searched instead for "street fight" and "kindness." The search for "street fight" resulted in

23.8 million videos, while "kindness" came in a distant second at almost two million hits.

So, why is our culture more interested in the harm done to people, instead of the kindness and compassion shown to our fellow man? Or is it that there is so much more violence than there is kindness? Surely it seems that way according to what we see on the news.

Do you personally benefit from hurting other people? Does it make you feel better when you put others down? Take a moment and write down a few negative things that you do that causes harm to others (e.g., yelling, talking behind people's back, bullying, etc.).

1.

2.

3.

4.

5.

Now, write down two reasons why you do those things.

1.

2.

Look back at your negatives. How would those things make you feel if you were on the receiving end? Do the two reasons you wrote down make you *and* the person you're being negative to happier people? In other words, are you both benefiting from your negative behavior? If not, then rethink your words and your actions.

Think of it in this way: Would you be okay if your conversations and attitudes toward people were broadcast on YouTube? If they were, would you get fired from your job? Would your family be ashamed of your actions? Would your friends be embarrassed to even say they know you? I know that's a lot of questions, but hopefully the point has gotten across. As before, I'm not telling you to live one way or the other. I just want you to think about the effect you have on others and whether or not you should change your negative behaviors. It's up to you and *only* you to make such changes.

Our environment has a big influence on our behaviors. For example, the problem might be that the people around you are negative. The easy solution would be to change your environment. However, that's not always possible. While it may not be possible to leave your environment, it is possible to shed a positive light on the surrounding darkness of negativity.

Hard? Yes.
Impossible? No.

It could also be that you've been the recipient of negative words and actions so many times that you decided to be a partaker and give it right back! If this is the case, you probably won't like chapter 6 where you come to find out that you can control your negativity/bad behaviors *no matter what someone else does to you.* I know it's not easy. It's certainly not easy staying positive around negative people, but it can be done.

It's important to note that one single positive or negative action toward someone could change his or her life for better or worse and you may never know it. That's right. One positive word or action could change someone's life forever.

I was cocky in high school right around the same time that the earth was orbiting around me. When you're cocky, you usually don't realize how arrogant or conceited you are to people. It just seems natural, right? Anyways, I walked around with an attitude of being better than other people even though I may not have thought much about who was paying attention.

An interesting thing happened to me about three years after I had graduated from high school. I received a message on Facebook from a girl I went to high school with who was a year older than me. Her message said, "What's with all the talk about God and quotes from scripture on your home page? I thought you were a real jackass in high school."

Cue the melting of my face and body in my chair.

Ouch.

I was speechless...or in this case, I was typeless. I had no immediate words or thoughts. Just shock and frustration. Frustration at myself.

And to make matters worse, I had never really spoke to or hung out with this person. All I could think about was the fact that I had had a negative influence on her and didn't even realize it. She was paying attention to my cocky attitude, selfishness, and unwelcoming spirit and it was hurtful to her. My selfish actions had a long-lasting *negative* impact on her.

This brings me to my next point:

There is always someone watching you and paying attention to your words and actions even if you don't know it. Make sure to be careful with your attitude and what you say. And take a moment to say a positive word to someone. You might help lift the person's spirits on a day that's not going very well for him or her.

Someone may even be looking up to you as a role model. If you are an encouragement and inspiration to people, think about how much good you can bring to those whom you may or may not know of who are watching you! The possibilities of positivity are endless.

Below, I have written out 107 positive changes that can be made on your OFY journey. Some changes do not directly affect other people, but are shaping you into a better person so that you can be happier and healthier, which in turn will allow you to influence and inspire other people to do the same! Please keep in mind that these are just suggestions. You have to be willing to commit to what's important to you! Chances are if you read through the list, you might find one that has already been in your heart to change, but haven't committed to changing it. Now is the time!

As you read through this list, highlight the ones that may have already been in your heart to change. Circle the ones that you may not have thought of that would be something you could change for the better.

107 Positive Changes for One Full Year

1) Don't text and drive.
2) Dating? Practice abstinence and grow on a more spiritual and emotional level.
3) Married? Be unselfish and fulfill the needs of your spouse.
4) Reconnect with an old friend.
5) Clean out the garage and get rid of *stuff*.
6) Volunteer in your community.
7) Find a widow and spend time visiting her and helping her in the community.
8) Kick a bad habit (smoking, cursing, excessive drinking, etc.).
9) Compliment your coworkers.
10) Call your friends and family instead of texting them.
11) Watch less TV.
12) Call your parents or grandparents more often.
13) Mentor an at-risk teen or inner-city child.
14) Foster or adopt a child.
15) Meditate daily/weekly.

16) Forgive a friend or family member who has caused you pain (reach out to him or her if it's been years).
17) Visit people in the hospital.
18) Take a deep breath and avoid road rage (yikes!).
19) Perform daily/weekly random acts of kindness (see website for more details).
20) Turn those random acts of kindness into *permanent* ones.
21) Be patient.
22) Give more time to your family instead of your electronic devices
23) Surprise your significant other every week.
24) Think through your words and actions before acting on them.
25) Write a book.
26) Write a song.
27) Deeply *study* the Bible.
28) Stop gossiping.
29) Sit down with a homeless person and listen to his or her story.
30) Get to know someone with a different race/ethnicity.
31) Quit complaining.
32) Donate to a struggling family.
33) Volunteer at a children's hospital.
34) Exercise.
35) Do something you've wanted to do, but have been afraid to do (go back to college, ride a

roller coaster, go skydiving, change careers, etc.).

36) Save money for a family vacation.

37) Put your phone down and build real, meaningful relationships with people.

38) No seriously, put your phone down.

39) Volunteer to babysit to give parents a date night

40) Take a break from social media or limit your time on it.

41) Learn a new skill.

42) Lose weight.

43) Praise children and then praise them some more.

44) Pay off your debt (or at least work toward it).

45) Send thank-you cards to local community heroes, such as teachers, police officers, firefighters, and so on.

46) Sit at the table beside the "uncool" kid.

47) Invite the "uncool" kid to your table.

48) Make better grades.

49) Count your blessings.

50) Be slow to anger.

51) Teach your children to share.

52) Unleash your inner beauty and see your outward beauty.

53) Stop bullying.

54) Give more than you receive.

55) Prepare meals for new moms, people who are sick, families who have lost someone close, and so on.

56) Be a comforter and not a condemner.

57) Go outside.

58) Mend a broken relationship with a family member or friend.

59) Share your story of redemption with people who have the same struggles.

60) Write a letter, call, or visit *everyone* who has had a positive impact on your *life*. (Don't worry, you have an entire year.)

61) Lend a helping hand (someone will always need one).

62) For all the people who you tell "I'll keep you in my prayers," actually pray for them or give them your time and assistance if possible.

63) Get along with your neighbors.

64) Tell others they're beautiful.

65) Start a charity or find one to donate to.

66) Pray with your spouse.

67) Eat healthier.

68) Adopt a pet.

69) Have a family game night once a week.

70) Swallow your pride (see #82).

71) Compare yourself to no one.

72) Hug more.

73) Help stranded drivers.

74) Control your temper.

75) Show good sportsmanship, whether you win or lose.

76) Lose an argument (or arguments).

77) Quit yelling.

78) Dads, give moms a break.

79) Find and start a new hobby.

80) Go on a mission trip.

81) Learn to swim (even if you're over fifty!).

82) Humble yourself (see #70).

83) Use your birthday money to donate to a local nonprofit that produces positive change in communities.

84) No more cheating.

85) Train for a marathon or triathlon

86) Get to work and other events on time (or even early).

87) Ride your bike to work. Be safe! (Part of my second OFY journey.)

88) Pick up trash in your neighborhood and community.

89) Be *involved* in a local church.

90) Share your wisdom humbly with others.

91) Stop bringing others down.

92) Take the stairs.

93) Donate blood, a kidney, or even bone marrow.

94) Be accepting of constructive criticism (even if it appears to be harsh).

95) Instead of donating old clothes/shoes/toys (which is great), give away something that will hurt.

96) Purify yourself from pornography.

97) Run a 5k/10k.

98) Go to college.

99) Invite a new coworker or neighbor over for dinner.

100) Learn to play an instrument.
101) Share your "getaway" home with a family in
     poverty or help pay for *their* vacation.
102) Cook meals for people who work on
     Thanksgiving, Christmas, or Easter.
103) Tutor a child for free.
104) Feed a family in poverty.
105) Update your social-media status to reflect
     goodness in others.
106) Mentor a prisoner.
107) Commit to and accomplish your OFY.

Insert your own here:

After reading the 107 Positive Changes list, I want
you to remember three very important things:

1) This list is not an all-inclusive list. There are
thousands of positive possibilities. It's very likely that
you already know what you're going to change.
Follow your heart and commit to it!

2) The purpose of your OFY journey is to change
for the better and change for life! For example, if you
choose to pick up trash in your neighborhood, it is
not a "one time and done" deal. Make it a habit for a
full year. And better yet, make it your end goal to

empower and influence your neighborhood and even local community to pick up trash monthly or bimonthly to create a healthier and more beautiful environment! How awesome would that be?

3) Even though your goal is to continue and build on your positive changes, there may be some positive actions you choose to do that may not last an entire year. For example, you may choose to donate a kidney. This would not last throughout a year. What makes donating a kidney part of your OFY is that when you recognize that someone needs a kidney (might be family, close friend, or a person you heard about on the news), and the thought crosses your mind to help, you go through with it. That's what makes this journey so great! You are choosing positive actions without hesitating or making excuses!

We all have the opportunity to make a difference.

The question is,

Will you make it a positive or negative one?

Chapter 4

What if I Fail?

Failure. One of the biggest and most terrifying fears we have that keeps us from accomplishing our goals is failure.

To fail simply means to not succeed.

While it is true that when a person fails he or she does not succeed in that moment, I do believe that failure can be turned into something positive that ultimately leads to our success. I want you to ask yourself this before you read any further, "Have you ever stopped trying because you failed or because you *feared* you would fail?"

Take a few minutes to reflect on all the things you want (or wanted) to accomplish that you gave up on due to failure or the fear of failing. At the top of the next page, write down a few of those things.

(Keep in mind that these things are not just physical goals such as exercising, but also mental and spiritual goals.)

Look at the list you made on this page or the things you thought of in your mind.

Why did you give up? Did someone tell you to? Did failure find you more times than you could handle?

Don't let failure stop you from accomplishing those goals and others. And don't worry about the times you have failed in the past. Let it go. Start fresh. Completely renew.

Failure is what kept me from writing this book for so long. Failure is what stopped me from my OFY journey for several years after the thought first crossed my mind. But all that changed when I changed how I look at failure. It all changed when I stopped being afraid of failure and started believing in success. It's easier to make positive changes for an entire year if you truly believe in yourself and realize your self-worth. You are worthy enough to accomplish whatever you put your mind to do. Don't let society's ridicule and criticism wear you down, and don't let your failures prevent you from your successes.

Let this statement resonate in your mind, "You will fail, but you are not a failure."

Did you get that?

You will fail, but you are not a failure!

The interesting thing though is that when you start your OFY journey, your mind-set should be *focused* on *not* failing. You should *forget to fail* and *remember to rise.* In other words, the idea of failing should not even cross your mind. I don't care how many times you've failed before; don't even think about it happening again.

Let me give you an example. Before starting my OFY journey, I would fail and tell myself I would do better and then fail again to the point where I would accept my failures as being a part of who I was. Every time I failed, I became more frustrated with myself which, in turn, would make me fail more often and with more ease. I eventually would give in to my failures and give up in even trying.

However, when I started my OFY journey, I put everything, and I mean everything, from my past in the past. I started completely fresh. I knew nothing of failure. I made an ongoing, daily, *conscious* effort to be my very best. I took one day at a time and focused solely on positive things. I had no fear of failing because my mind was trained to *only* think I would succeed.

As humans we are going to fail. No matter how hard we try, we are going to fail at some point in our life...and more than once. The problem is not that we fail; it's what we do next. A lot of the time we let our failures define who we are.

People try to overcome certain behaviors, but they fail over and over to the point where they give up. As a real-life example, several smokers have told me that giving up cigarettes is very hard. I've never smoked, but I believe them because most bad habits are hard to quit, especially if you've been doing it for several years. The sad part though is that most of them would just tell me they have tried to quit and can't do it. Some have said they're going to die eventually, so it might as well be by smoking. (I have seen many smokers in the hospital. The later years of their life is very difficult and miserable.)

They let their failures define them and become them. Most of them knew that smoking was a bad habit. They knew that it wasn't beneficial to their health or positive to their overall well-being, but they chose to give up and give in.

I don't mean to pick on smokers. All of us have bad habits that we've given in to. But don't let a bad habit become you. Don't continue in your bad habit and never let go of the opportunities to break it. If you have a bad habit, choose to fight and overcome during OFY and enjoy the freedom of your victory.

I have heard a lot of people say, "That's just who I am" in referring to a negative behavior that has been instilled in their character. They have seen their parents do it, or a best friend, and so on. They have been surrounded by the negative behavior throughout their lives and they have let it define them as a person.

Does this describe you? Have you fought with something for so long that you finally gave in and admitted to yourself that it's "just who you are?"

Let me tell you, "It's not who you are!"

You are strong enough not to settle and succumb to negative behaviors.

I read a post by a man who said he had been struggling with something for a long time. He said that he knew in his heart that his struggle was hurting his life and causing him grief, stress, and hardship. He went on to say that after fighting the struggle and constantly failing, he gave in. He let that struggle become a part of him.

Maybe you feel like this man. Maybe you feel like you have failed so much that there's no point of redemption. The truth of the matter is that you can absolutely be redeemed. You can absolutely overcome and change for the better. Find someone who has been through the same struggles who can give you guidance and support. Once you have conquered your previous failures, you can kindly and compassionately lend a helping hand to someone who is going through the same battles that you have defeated.

As this chapter concludes, you may have one burning question in your mind.

"Did I fail at any point throughout my OFY journey?"

And the answer is yes.

About four months into my OFY challenge, I had a bad week. I got into several arguments with my wife where I was raising my voice out of anger (one of my challenges was to have patience with her and have control over my temper), and I made some other bad choices.

All in one week.

But you know what I did? I did something that I had never done before. I didn't lay there and wallow in my failures. I forgot about it, and I doubled down. I picked myself up quickly and worked even harder on my challenges. During the next eight months, I was more focused than ever before on making positive changes. It became easier and more exciting every time I succeeded. I can proudly say that I accomplished my goals because I did not let one bad week mess up an *entire* year's worth of positive change. I learned from it and dedicated more time and effort to my OFY journey and *you* can do the exact same thing.

I believe too often that we give up too easily. We let the "devil" on our shoulder win. The devil tells us it's so much easier to just accept the fact that we're not good enough. This time the devil loses. This time you crowd and overwhelm yourself with positive people, positive influences, and positive words that can make you successful in your journey to be better.

Believing you can do something is always healthier and more positive than worrying that you will fail. It doesn't matter where you're at or where you've been, you can overcome. You have the capability to change for the better. But you have to find the determination and willpower to push through your past and focus on a brighter and better future.

Oh, and this is the shortest chapter in this book. It was intentionally written short and to the point.

Why?

Because it's much healthier to focus on success and all the positive things in your life instead of remembering your failures. Refocus your thoughts on all the good you can accomplish in your lifetime. The possibilities are endless and your talents are plenty.

As you read the final statements of this chapter located on the next page, take every word to heart. Write them down. Put reminders on your phone. Make Post-it notes and pin them to your fridge. Fill your life with these words and many other positive and inspiring images, music, and people. Do whatever it takes to overcome this time and change for the better.

Be courageous.

Be strong.

Believe in your changes.

Believe in your journey.

Forget to fail.

Remember to rise.

84 Believe in Your Changes

Success Starts Here

1) You've come this far because you know there are positive changes you want to make. Nothing in this book or words anywhere else can make you take the first step. It's completely up to you. Take a leap of faith and commit to your One Full Year!

2) Deep within us we all want the hero to win. We long for good to defeat evil. Today, tomorrow, the rest of your OFY, and your life, you are the hero.

3) If you love music, make an inspirational playlist of songs. Music has long been a part of my life and has helped me get through the most trying and difficult times in my life. I made a playlist to encourage and uplift me on my journey. (Audiomachine, Hans Zimmer, Mark Mancina, and Collective Soul are among my favorites!) Find positive music to inspire you to keep going! (And on the other hand, eliminate music that has a negative effect on you.)

4) Eliminate things that get in the way and take up your time. While it's important to fill your life with positive and healthy thoughts and people during your journey, it's equally important to give up some stuff that might not necessarily fall into the negative category. For example, if you have to wake up earlier, watch less sports, or change your daily routine, then don't be afraid to do so.

5) Choose your Trusted and Loyal Companion, or TALC for short, and write a letter to him or her. When I started my OFY, I wrote a letter to the person I trusted the most, the person who I felt closest to and did not want to disappoint. So, I wrote a letter to my wife. In this letter, I explained my OFY journey—what my purpose was and what I wanted to accomplish. I sealed it in an envelope and labeled it to be opened exactly one year from the start of my OFY. I knew that everything I wanted to accomplish was sealed away, and it would come to light at the end of my year. This helped me stay focused on my goals because I knew she would read the letter, and then we would discuss the results of my journey.

At times throughout my first OFY, I was tempted to give in and fail. But then I thought about that letter and the words that I had written to my wife. No way was I going to let her down. So, those temptations to fail became easier to defeat. When we sat down to discuss the letter, she told me that she knew I was working on peace, patience, and my temper. She could see those changes in me. It was a glorious moment for us! After much discussion about OFY, my wife set out on her own journey. She wrote me a letter and gave it to me, but I can already see some of her changes without even knowing exactly what they are!

Find someone whom you completely trust and would not want to disappoint no matter the cost. Write them a letter containing your OFY journey. Seal it and give it to them with the opening date on the label—a year from your OFY start date. Tell that person to hide it in a place that only he or she knows where it is. Maybe your TALC will be doing their own OFY and you can exchange envelopes. If not, and your TALC asks you what the envelope is all about, tell your TALC you're on a personal journey describing what OFY is, but don't disclose the details.

Don't have a TALC?

Send your letter to OFY at the address listed at the end of this book. Just write the start date of your OFY on the side where the envelope is sealed. We will keep your letter unopened for an entire year and check in with you throughout the year to see how things are going.

It's interesting to note that the mineral Talc is the softest mineral on the planet. Hopefully, your TALC will possess the same characteristic by having a *soft* heart. Soft-hearted people are kind, gentle, and compassionate. If we could be a little more like this, we could make a huge, positive impact in the lives of people. If you are chosen to be someone's TALC, be awesome and show your softer, more forgiving and loving side!

One important note: If you need a mentor/accountability partner to help with your OFY, please find one. You can still write to your TALC, while sharing your OFY with an accountability partner. For example, maybe you're a husband and you want to help your wife with house chores for an entire year by cooking two to three times a week, vacuuming weekly, or helping with laundry. You talk with your friend who is also married and you both decide to commit to the same thing while encouraging each other and holding each other accountable. That's perfect. You can still write a letter to your spouse if you choose to do so.

What if your accountability partner is your TALC? In this case, you can either write a letter together to someone you both trust or you can forego the letter and support one another in your journey.

If it's a spiritual matter, you should find a friend, minister, or elder who is strong in the faith to guide you and pray for you. If this is the case, you can still write a letter to someone close to you other than the person who knows your spiritual struggle. This way, you will have a double dose of accountability which will strengthen your desire to renew. You can also collaborate with your church or small group and determine a OFY goal to help the community or challenge one another to develop a deeper faith in Christ. You can even plan events throughout the year to grow closer in your relationships with one another. Spiritual matters such as these are definitely great things to change throughout your OFY and may not require writing any letters to your TALC.

6) Read chapter 7. Believe in it and dedicate your time to it.

Chapter 5

Well, Look at the Time

Time is one of the most precious commodities in our human life that cannot be bought. Everything we do in life is based on time. Work, play, sleep, eating...all are confined to time. We never have enough of it and always seem to need more.

But as the saying goes, "Time waits for no man."

So, why did I find it necessary to dedicate a whole chapter to the subject of time? Because it seems that time, or the lack thereof, is one of the biggest excuses we make when it comes to making positive changes. When it comes to making ourselves better and serving others, we just can't seem to find the time. However, I truly believe that we have enough time to do everything we need to do...and more. I believe we have enough time to better ourselves and each other. The problem is that we don't know how to prioritize our time.

Let me give you a very simple example.

About eight years ago, I decided that I was going to start working out. I had played sports all of my life, but I was starting to get out of shape, and I wanted to get leaner, build some muscle, and be healthier altogether. I worked out consistently for three months and then quit. I never went back to the gym. I decided that I was "too busy," and I didn't have enough time to drive to a gym that was open 24–7 and work out. As I started to analyze my time, I realized that I wasn't near as busy as I thought. Most of my time was going to video games, extra sleep, watching TV, surfing the Internet, and basically just lounging around. The truth is that I had *plenty* of time to work out; I just used my time to do other things that had no benefit to my overall well-being. Now, I'm not saying there is anything wrong with video games and the other aforementioned items, but they don't help us grow spiritually, physically, or mentally. You know if you're spending too much time indulging in those things and just being plain lazy.

This is just one example. I have countless other examples that I couldn't even fit into this entire book. The point is that I have wasted so much time that I could have used to make myself better and reach out to others who were in need of compassion.

Have you ever said you were too busy to help someone or be productive when you've actually binge-watched ten hours of *The Walking Dead* or some other popular TV show? If you're smiling right now, it probably means you have.

Am I saying that you need to give up your favorite TV shows? Sort of. I'm saying you should focus on your OFY changes first, and then if you have time, you can watch your TV show. If you watch TV first and put off your changes, you may *never* have the time to change.

Some Opportunities May Knock Only Once

I wouldn't necessarily say that I've had regrets in life. I view "regrets" as learning experiences. But as I've gotten older, I have looked back on my days in high school and college, and I wish I had seized certain opportunities that were laid out before me.

For example, I saw a lot of people who were "alone." People who were lost. People who were broken. But, for the most part, I didn't go to them. I didn't stop and talk to them. I didn't give them any of my time because I had more important things to do and places to be...or did I?

What would have happened if I reached out to those people *every* time I saw someone in that position? How would their lives have changed if I gave them just a few minutes of my time to let them know that I care? Better yet, how would my life have changed for the better if I had talked to them?

Have you ever seen someone hurting and alone and made the decision to walk right past that person? Or did you pretend that you didn't see them?

There are a lot of people who feel broken and alone because they don't "fit in" anywhere. Maybe they don't feel a sense of belonging. Maybe they are away from family and friends for the first time. Maybe they lost a family member or maybe they have cancer.

Most of the time we don't know any of these things to be true or not because we think we are too busy and even too important to give someone our time and our listening ear.

Most of the time when we are presented with an opportunity to make a positive difference, we pass on the chance thinking that we can do it another time, only to realize at a later time that that moment was the *only* time.

Take hold of every opportunity because it might be the only one you'll ever have.

One of the most humbling experiences I've ever had in my life is the time that I got up two hours before the break of dawn to assemble with a small group in Memphis, Tennessee to search out and find the homeless. It was our mission to seek them out and talk with them to find out what their needs were.

I went to some of the "scariest" places in Memphis early that morning: dark alleys, underneath bridges, open fields, and abandoned buildings.

The group that I was searching with found a man who we'll call George.

I sat down with George on a concrete slab in the parking lot of an old shopping center. I asked him questions, and I listened to his answers. He told me he previously had a place to live and a full-time job until he made some poor choices and lost everything. George then traveled from city to city hitching rides mostly from truck drivers. He was searching, but he wasn't sure what he was searching for. George knew his bad choices had put him in his current situation, and he wasn't afraid to admit that. After I had asked him what his needs were and we had talked for a moment, he became emotional, shook my hand, and with a faint smile said, "Thanks."

But why was he thankful? I hadn't given him money or food. Matter of fact, I hadn't given him anything. But right before I left, I realized why he was thankful. He was thankful because I took the time to sit down with him and talk to him like he was any other person.

Like he was my best friend.

I didn't shame him or make fun of him. I didn't tell him he was filthy or abhor him for making bad decisions. I talked to him, I listened to him, and I gave him my time. More often than not, that's what people need. They need our time and our compassion. Not money. Not a handout. Just quality time spent with them.

The ironic thing is that George did more for me than I did for him that early morning in Memphis. He taught me the power of human connection. The power of communication and listening to one another. The power of *time* spent with others.

The point is that we have time to do positive things, but we *choose* not to. And the funny thing is that most of what we should be doing may only take us about thirty minutes to an hour to complete.

How many times have you gotten on YouTube or some other website to look at a video that your friend told you about, and before you know it, you've spent over two hours clicking on videos to the point of where you're now watching a cat "play" the piano while a dog "sings" in the background? It happens. It's happened to me, and I'm sure it's happened to you.

We do the same thing with social media as well. Think about how many times you have flipped through your Facebook feed for minutes, sometimes hours at a time. The CEO of Facebook, Mark

Zuckerberg, stated in 2016 that the average US consumer spends an average of fifty minutes on Facebook per day![2] Almost a full hour per day! That equals an average of 350 minutes per week or almost six hours. Think about what you could do with an extra five to six hours per week! And you may even spend more time on it than that!

While the Internet and our computer can be of great benefit to us, we often spend countless hours of wasted time using them. It's probably safe to say that most of you reading this have spent or do spend a great deal of time surfing the Internet. And once again, while some of that time spent is beneficial, for the most part, it's an absolute big waste of time. Watching countless hours of videos on YouTube or flipping through posts on Facebook don't do us much good.

We have consumed so much of our lives with electronic devices that we don't even know how to connect with each other. We have a hard time building relationships. Better yet, we have a hard time building *authentic* relationships with each other.

Remember George from earlier? The greatest gift I gave him was my time. And it was only a few minutes. It's probably safe to assume that George didn't have Facebook either. The only way to connect with him was to seek him out and have a real face-to-face conversation with him. What if you used some of your time to seek out people in need? What if you took your time to build meaningful and positive relationships with your neighbors, acquaintances, or people who are of a different race from you?

Time is very important to completing your OFY challenge. You will have to learn to redirect your time into purposeful and positive actions.

One of the challenges in my OFY was to call my grandparents more often. I say more often, but the fact of the matter is that I hardly called them at all. Why? Well, I mostly blamed it on time. I was too busy. But I really wasn't. Once I started to call them, I realized that each phone call only lasted about fifteen to twenty minutes. I'm not telling you that to say that there wasn't much to say to them or that I'm glad our calls didn't take an hour. I am saying that because I had that much time and more every week to talk to them. In the past, I told myself that I was too busy so I could use that as an excuse for not calling. And so it goes with most everything in life.

In one of my calls to my grandma, I asked her for the recipe to the goulashes she used to make us grandkids when we were younger. I told her that I was sorry for calling and bothering her just to ask about a recipe. She then told me, "I love it when you call and need me. You can ask me for anything."

Just a simple phone call about a recipe made her day, as it did mine.

I wonder how often we tell people that we're busy and then stop and realize that we're not as busy as we think we are.

It's probably safe to say that the phrase, "I'm too busy," is our number-one excuse for not taking time for others. I can honestly admit that I have said that phrase several times in my life and not actually meant it. I have used those words to get out of helping and spending time with others. We all have.

Don't make the excuse to someone that you're too busy if you're truly not. Make time for others, and then make time for you. You will probably be more blessed and glad that you did!

We often wonder why we are stressed and unhappy people. I truly believe one of those reasons is because we make poor use of our time, and I think that if you stop for a minute and think about where your time goes, you would agree with me.

Some of you may not struggle with prioritizing your time. Some of you may schedule your time for your kids, work, school projects, volunteering, and so on, and have read through this chapter and think that you don't have an extra minute to add anything to your busy life.

However, I still feel it necessary for you to examine your amount of time each day and see if you can make better use out of what you have.

I also know that the amount of time that each of us have on this earth is different. If everything else in this book is mostly opinion, there is absolutely one fact I can share with you:

We are all going to die one day.

Now, I don't want to bring up death to focus your attention on something negative. But since we are on the chapter of time, I thought it would be a good idea to remind you that our time on earth is limited. Some of us have eighty years, while some of us have twenty years. Regardless of how many days you are given on this earth, you have to make the most of your time right now.

Not tomorrow. Right now.

Don't put things off and think that you will have another day. The longer you put something off, the less time you will have to do it. And it's more likely that you will never do it. The last thing you want to do is wait on making some amazing and wonderful changes in your life only to find out that you don't have as much time as you need. And, on the other hand, someone may pass from this life before you get a chance to make things right with them or before you were able to make a positive difference in their life.

No matter how much time we have on this earth, we have to make a *conscious* effort to make the absolute best of it. We can all be better. We can all make a positive difference right now, right where we are, and it starts with prioritizing your time better.

After reading this chapter, stop and think about how you spend your time.

Do you waste time? Do you have more time throughout the week than you realized? Are you using your time in a positive and beneficial way?

Reflect on these questions and how you value time before starting the next chapter.

On the next page, write down where you spend most of your time in any given day. Make a list or a chart that shows where your time is spent. As you make your list, write out beside each item if time spent in this activity is beneficial and positive and if you should give more or less time to that particular activity.

Remember, if you want to accomplish your goals, you may have to eliminate certain things from your life. It won't be the end of the world if you have to wait a day or two before you can watch your favorite show. It certainly won't hurt to take some time away from playing on your phone or computer. Sometimes the things we think make us the most happy, actually leave us feeling empty and stressed.

Keep in mind that our time is limited on this earth, so make the most out of every minute you have.

Where I spend most of my time on any given day:

Activities I could give more time to:

Activities I can take time from:

Once you've evaluated your time, think very seriously about how to prioritize it because time is a very precious thing to waste. Don't wait until tomorrow to realize how important it is to spend more time with your family, spend more time serving others, and spend more time making positive changes in your life.

Final Thought

If *everyone in the world* gave *only* one minute of *his or her time* in any given day to show kindness and compassion to their neighbor, or to commit to their positive changes, that would equate to about 13,318 years of kindness and positive change in a single day.

Chapter 6

You Always Have a Choice

Before you read this chapter, please make note of the following: I understand and am well aware of the fact that there are certain terrible and horrific things that a person can be forced to do against his or her will (e.g., rape, child molestation, sex trafficking, etc.). If you have been a victim of any these heinous acts, I am truly sorry. I hope and pray that you have found strength and renewal through those difficult times in your life. You are a brave and strong person. You are beautiful inside and out and no one can take that from you.

With that being said, this chapter deals with those things of which we do have control. It deals with choices that we make every day of our lives. And yes, we do make decisions every...single...day.

We choose what clothes to wear, what to eat, what time to go to work, when to wake up, how much TV to watch, how fast to drive, what words to say, and the list goes on and on.

Bottom line: We choose how we live, and those choices have an effect on people around us, even more so than we realize.

For example, when you drive your car, your speed, turning, and braking affects the other drivers around you. When you go to a restaurant and order food, someone behind you in line will have to wait a few extra minutes. Furthermore, when you buy the last concert tickets or book the last hotel room, someone else is frantically searching for other options. Do you even think about these actions altering someone else's plans? Probably not. And that's okay. They're not very important things to be concerned with in the grand scheme of life. However, there are a lot of choices you make that are important and can have a lasting impact on your life and the life of others.

In order to make positive changes on an emotional, mental, and spiritual level, you must practice self-discipline and learn to control your actions in a world where you have *no control* over other people's behavior and *complete control* of your own.

For example, you may yell at your spouse during an argument and when your spouse asks why you're yelling, you may respond,

"Because you yelled first," or

"Because I'm tired of you leaving dirty laundry on the floor," or

"Because I do all the work around this house."

The list goes on.

We try to justify our yelling and harsh language because our spouse did something we didn't like. But here's the deal. *You can respond calmly, kindly, and lovingly every single time. You can always control your words and actions no matter what!* I'll give you a moment while you reread that statement and contemplate whether or not you think I'm in my right mind.

Close your eyes.

Take a deep breath.

Exhale.

All right. Better now? (If not, take another deep breath...or two.)

The first thing going through *your mind* might be this:

I have no idea of the type of people you work with, or how verbally abusive a peer, a parent, or even a spouse might be to you.

And you would be right.

I honestly don't know what kind of people you deal with on a daily basis. However, if you were honest with yourself, you would realize that you could probably do a better job of controlling your negative actions and words toward those types of people. I'm not saying that you let people bully you, abuse you, or walk all over you. What I am saying, and want you to understand, is that you *can* control what you say and do...nobody makes you do it.

You always have a choice on how you react and respond to people. Whether it be a friend, a parent, a coworker, or your worst enemy, you can train yourself to say the right words, use the correct tone of voice, and ultimately control your anger.

"What's the fun in that?"

"I'm too old and worn out to care what people think!"

"It's much easier to blow my top instead of letting people run all over me!"

Is this how you currently feel? Is this the attitude you've had in regards to how you respond to people who do "stupid" things or talk down to you?

From my experience, this type of thinking doesn't solve problems and for sure it doesn't build anyone up. And, if you're honest with yourself, it doesn't make you feel much better...or maybe it does. Maybe you feel better by talking bad about people behind their back. Maybe by bringing others down as low as possible to your friends and peers, you build yourself up.

Pause for a quick-thought question: If someone came up to you and said, "I'm going to steal your identity and most of your assets by the end of the month," how would you respond?

Would you respond by telling them, "That's fine with me" and continue as if it didn't matter? Or would you take immediate action and report this person to the cops?

Take five seconds to think about

this...

and...

time.

You would immediately report that person, right?

Because this person would be profiting or building him- or herself up at the expense of your hard work.

So why do we do the exact same thing with our words? Why is it okay to steal a person's dignity to build up ourselves? Why is okay to strip someone of his or her humanity just so we can look better in front of our peers?

Take a brief moment and answer the questions above. Patience with people who "get on your nerves" can be very challenging, but it can be done, and it's so much more beneficial to you and that person when you show compassion and kindness. Even when it hurts to do so.

Let's touch on the concept of controlling your anger. Let me be clear:

There is nothing wrong with being angry.

One more time: There is nothing wrong with expressing anger.

There is, however, a certain point at which you let your anger boil over until it has no benefit and is completely harmful to its intended receiver. And no matter how people treat you, you have the ability to respond with love and respect every single time.

Let me give you a personal example. As I mentioned briefly in chapter 4, I have a temper. It doesn't come around often, but it's there nonetheless. When I first got married, I didn't know how to control my temper, nor did I even care to. My temper was like an angry, barking dog pulling at its owner from the leash and when it came time for me to choose a calmer path or a path of outrage, I would let the leash go. Once it started, I didn't care what I said or how badly I hurt my wife with my words. It seemed as though my goal was to belittle and deprecate her until I felt "high and mighty."

I don't know if that works for you, but it has *never* worked for me. I finally decided to get a hold of my temper after looking back on each incident and realizing there was *never* a positive outcome after my outbursts.

Never.

As I stated earlier, during my first OFY journey, I decided to work on controlling that temper by being more patient and listening to the concerns and needs of my wife. Throughout my journey, I had to learn how to control my tongue, take deep breaths, assess my thoughts (before they became actions), and let stuff roll off my back. It was not easy, but it made for a much better marriage.

It was easier to have a healthy discussion about things we disagreed on, and express anger without blowing a top. There were still times that my wife made me mad, and I wanted to unleash my temper, but I made *conscious* efforts to control it. I was not perfect, but controlling my temper was much better. I still have to be mindful to keep my temper in check. I am well aware that this will be an ongoing effort for as long as my days are on this earth.

Remember, your OFY journey is not to last only a year. If controlling your temper is a part of your OFY, you will have to practice self-control every year after your first OFY ends. Hopefully, these positive changes will get easier and easier the more you practice them. Your end goal is to allow your changes to help you live a happier and more fulfilling life, which will enable you to bring about the good in others and ultimately influence people to commit to their own positive changes for an entire year.

Not My Fault!

One of the biggest reasons for writing this chapter is to discuss the bad habit of blaming others for our actions. As I have observed people and talked to them about what gets in the way of making changes and being a better person, blaming others is one of the excuses at the top of the list. Here are just a few thoughts I've heard or seen:

"I just can't stand Amy. She makes me so mad. Every time she's around I just want to punch her in the face!"

"I can't help that I yell and have a temper. I get that from my dad."

You've had a bad day at work so you get home and take it out on your family.

"That car cut me off. I'm going to run it off the road and give them the finger!"

My personal favorite: "If it wasn't for President Clinton, Bush, Obama, Trump, Reagan, Taft, Fillmore, and so on, this country wouldn't be in such a mess!"

Truthfully, it's not in a mess. We're beyond blessed to live in a country where we can enjoy the freedom and opportunities that have been fought for and given to us.

Sure, it's not perfect. But we could strive for perfection if we all quit placing blame on everyone else and start finding ways that *we* can make it better. Be the solution, not the problem. Bring about goodwill and happiness to others. Focus on positive change and let's quit with the blame game! (Wow, that was a cheesy rhyme—but effective, I think!)

Instead of constantly blaming people, ask yourself what you can do to bring about positive change. It starts with changing yourself. It continues with encouraging, uplifting, and serving others.

You can still talk to "Amy" with a smile on your face. Or politely avoid confrontation if that's for the better.

Don't blame your parents for your lack of self-control. No matter what they did, you can choose to be different. You can *always* make *better* choices.

De-stress your mind and body before you get home so your attitude will be much better. Otherwise, the entire family will be in a bad mood.

Even though the car cut you off, take a deep breath and go on. It doesn't matter in the grand scheme of life. It won't even matter ten seconds from when it happened.

If you're starting to think that I'm expecting you to be pleasant all the time in every situation, you're mistaken. We are all human, and humans aren't perfect. But I want you to understand that you do have a choice in every situation. Train yourself to believe that you can choose good thoughts and kind words no matter the circumstances.

Learn to own up to *your* mistakes.

As a human race, we do a very poor job of taking responsibility for our own actions, and yes, this includes me too. On more than one occasion, I have made the choice to point out the mistakes of other people to justify my wrongdoings. I've tried to make my mistake look minor compared to someone else's *past* mistakes. Owning up to our mistakes is very hard, especially when pride gets in the way, but it makes us more humble and strong individuals. The other side of that coin never looks very good. Bringing up someone else's mistakes only belittles that person, and it never solves our own problems.

Our society is full of stories where people are blaming someone else for their mistake. Every time a Republican makes a mistake, it's the Democrats' fault, and vice versa. This only creates more hatred and more division. Many more examples such as this exist in our society and you probably know what they are without me listing them here.

Sometimes we jump right in the middle of the discussion, creating more problems and discord. During the 2016 US presidential election, I couldn't tell you how many times I heard someone say that he or she was getting so upset and frustrated with the online political war that was taking place on social media.

There is no doubt that people can say things that anger us, no matter where you stand. However, taking a break from social media is just one of the many solutions to avoid getting upset at such things. Instead, *we choose* to continue listening to or reading such negative posts, which causes us to get angrier and more frustrated. And, as mentioned above, we decide to join the conversation with our hateful words and finger-pointing which accomplishes nothing. Especially nothing positive.

Once again, our choices, not the words of people on social media, bring sadness and gloom into our lives. Yes, seeing other people say and do negative things can bring us down, but we can *choose positive actions to inspire positive solutions* in a negative environment.

Everyone Has a Special Lens

We look at the world through a "special" lens. This "special" lens allows us to see everyone else's problems with perfect twenty-twenty vision! We are able to see the imperfection in other people—their bad attitude, their marital problems, their dirty clothes and unkempt hair, and the list goes on. This lens even has the power to make us feel really good about ourselves since we can see how bad other people's lives are. Thank goodness we all have been given this lens to view people in a negative light!

Catching the sarcasm yet?

While this lens doesn't necessarily blame others for our actions, it puts others down for our own glory. It creates a quick judgment of someone before we even know anything about him or her.

I'll be the first to admit that I used to judge a person and *think* I had him or her all figured out in the first few minutes of making *only* eye contact.

"That person has a bunch of tattoos; he must be a misfit or a felon."

"That person on TV is protesting during the day; why doesn't she go get a job?"

"That person is really fat; he needs to lay off the fast food."

And so on and so forth.

I was wrong for doing that. Did I know his or her life story? Did the person with tattoos volunteer at a local shelter? Did the protestor work throughout the night? Is the fat person currently on a diet? How would I know since I didn't spend time talking to and building a relationship with that person?

Is this currently how you think? Do you automatically push someone aside or avoid talking to him or her because you think you've got him or her figured out? Are you *quick* to judge someone based on what you see?

In the hospital on one of the units was a small whiteboard displaying a short message that had a major impact on my way of thinking.

It simply said this:

"Everyone is fighting a battle you know nothing about."

What would happen if you treated everyone with compassion first, and then when you found out more about him or her, you could treat that person with even more compassion? See what I did there?

Have you taken the time lately to talk to someone who is *different* from you to know what battles he or she has faced or is currently going through? What would happen if you met people on their level instead of asking them to come up to where you are? Instead of using other people's misery, mistakes, and despair to build up yourself, how about finding a way to comfort and support them through their difficult situation?

Think about it.

Think about the positive influence you could have on someone if you humbled yourself and listened to his or her story. Maybe his or her story would have more of a positive influence on you than you could have imagined.

Think about making this a part of your OFY.

You *always* have a choice to be better. You *always* have a choice to help improve the lives of others. You *always* have a choice to inspire and uplift people. You *always* have a choice to make a positive impact on the world.

You know the golden rule? Do unto others as you would have them do unto you. You've probably heard that a thousand times, right? Let's change it just a bit:

"Do good unto others no matter

what they do unto you."

Too challenging? That's the purpose of OFY.

Too hard? More than likely.

Impossible? No.

Remember, you always have a choice.

What will you choose?

Chapter 7

The Power of Prayer

Prayer: An address (as a petition) to God or a god in word or thought.[3]

We hear about prayer all the time. Whether you are a Christian or not, the idea of prayer is everywhere.

"Our thoughts and prayers are with the victims" may be one of the most familiar phrases we hear after a natural disaster, terrorist act, or terrible crime. Is it something we say just to make people feel better? Are we putting forth effort to personally reach out to those who are hurting? If we are telling people we will "pray for them," are we actually doing that? Better yet, is it possible for you to provide direct assistance to that person, instead of just saying "I'll keep you in my prayers?" More thoughts on this later.

So what does it actually mean to pray, and why is prayer significant to your OFY journey?

If you don't believe in prayer or have prayed before but don't think God is listening, skip to page

129. Otherwise, take a leap of faith and keep reading.

Why Prayer?

As a Christian, I have "prayed" all my life. Why? Because that's what Christians are supposed to do and because my parents told me to. Wrong and wrong. It isn't until you fully understand prayer and its power that you come to realize the importance it plays in your life and in the life of the people you are praying for.

We pray because we trust in an all-powerful, loving, just, and merciful God to help us through the seemingly impossible and most difficult times in our life. We also pray to thank Him for the goodness and the blessings He has given us, which are evident in our everyday lives!

Take a quick moment and jot down a few of the blessings you have received from God.

Blessings are certainly good, but are earthly blessings the reason you pray? Are you reaching out to God only in the bad times? Do you even thank

Him for all the good moments in your life, even the undeserving air you breathe daily?

We have to pray knowing that we might not like the answer. I used to pray only when I *needed* God in difficult times. And, to be quite *real* with you, I finished my prayers believing that God would give me what *I* wanted. Did you catch that? I prayed for what *I* wanted. Not what God knew was best. The result I wanted is whatever would make me the happiest and make me feel the most comfortable.

Have you ever prayed like that or do you currently pray like that? Do you pray for God's help and then hope that He gives you what you want? Maybe you pray for something but hope that God will allow you to stay in your "comfort zone."

During my OFY journey, I stepped up my prayer game. I decided to pray often. I decided to pray that God give me wisdom. I prayed for God to direct my path. I prayed for God to use me in a way that would glorify Him, influence people to live better lives, and ultimately lead people to become a part of His kingdom. The difference for me this time is that I meant it. I finished my prayers accepting God's will for me. I was at peace knowing that God may want me to step out of my comfort zone, and in a big way. I was at peace knowing that God may want me to serve in ways that I would have refused to do just a few years ago. I was at peace fully believing and trusting in a Creator who gives me my every breath.

But I wasn't always there. As a matter of fact, I was far from that. I used to be afraid to put my full faith and trust in Him because I was fearful of what He might want me to do!

In other words, I wasn't ready to fully follow Him. I wasn't ready *to fully commit* to *His will.* So, how did I get ready?

Well, it all started in the spring of 2009.

I started college in the fall of 2004 at UCA in Conway, Arkansas. I had just graduated high school with a 4.07 weighted GPA, which was good enough for seventh in my graduating class. I came to college with the intention of continuing that trend (after all, I had never made a C and only a couple of Bs). Within the first semester, I realized quickly that college was going to be a lot harder than high school. Even so, I finished my first year with all As and Bs.

Fast-forward to the end of my third semester of college. I was taking a final exam in a business-statistics class when my life changed forever.

While I don't admit to being a very smart person, I do love numbers, and statistics is right up my alley. Before the final exam, I had made all As in the class that included two tests and a lot of homework. I even managed to obtain a few bonus points. Only problem was that there wasn't a whole lot of total points in the class, so I knew the final exam would be worth a lot toward my overall grade.

After the test was handed out, I worked through the first couple of problems without much hesitation and then I went in to full panic mode. All of a sudden, I couldn't recall anything. I don't know if you've ever had this experience before, but it's one of the worst feelings when taking a test. The rest of the test looked foreign to me. I started to look around the room to see if everyone else had blank stares on their face like me, but I didn't notice anything unusual. I looked back down at my test hoping to recall something, but I couldn't. I fixed a stare up on the wall in the front of the room near the teacher, hoping to pull something out of thin air. Still nothing. I looked up again, and this time I noticed something that caught my eye.

A fellow classmate, who was sitting two rows to my right, kept looking down toward her seat and then back to her test paper.

I looked away from her and then back to my paper.

I looked back at her, and she was still looking back and forth from her seat to her test paper. Then I noticed what was going on. My classmate had positioned an index card underneath her legs and was using it to get the answers to the test. She was cheating, and it was now obvious to me. But she was being very crafty about it.

Since I was still in panic mode with no recollection of how to work the problems, I decided to keep an eye on her. My classmate was waiting until another student would walk in front of the teacher's desk and temporarily block the teacher's view of the class. Then she would reveal the card to see the answers and then hide the card as soon as the student walked away.

If you have never experienced panic and anger at the same time during a final exam, count yourself lucky. I was sweating and infuriated at the same time!

I finally finished the test, putting random thoughts that surfaced into my mind on my paper. The results of the test came in and unsurprisingly to me, I had failed the exam. This result gave me my very first overall C."

If you're reading this and thinking, "He ranted on and on just to tell me he got his first C as a sophomore in college...and to think that I got my first C in middle school?"

Just wait. There's a lot more to this story.

At the end of that year, I lost my scholarship. And because of the anger I felt toward that student for blatantly cheating, on top of failing my test, and ultimately losing my scholarship, I started to cheat the following year. I didn't cheat in every class, and I didn't even cheat that often, but I did nonetheless.

Fast-forward about three years later to 2008.

In the summer of that year, I got accepted into the occupational-therapy program, a graduate-level program at the ripe ole age of twenty-two.

In the fall semester of 2008, I was still cheating into grad school and, quite honestly, just being lazy. The cheating wasn't as prevalent, but it was still happening. At this point, I was more concerned with hanging out with friends and playing sports. I really wasn't ready for graduate-level coursework, but I'll be the first to admit that even though twenty-two is young, it's no excuse for laziness and not putting forth much effort in a graduate-level program or any level of coursework, for that matter.

Now the beginning of what was to come:

It was spring semester of 2009, my second semester of graduate studies.

Around March of this semester, I decided it was time for a change. I started praying to God that I would stop cheating, start working harder, and dedicate more time to my studies. Most of my prayers included, "God, please help me focus on my studies and work harder in each of my classes. Help me do honest work, no matter what it takes."

My prayers were focused on God helping me overcome my bad habit of cheating no matter the cost.

The problem is that sometimes when we pray for something, we want *our will* to be done. We pray and hope that God will grant us the easy way out. While that was my attitude in a lot of my previous prayers, it was different and humbling this time.

So I started studying more, reading more, and praying more. I was finally at peace with praying to God that He help me stop cheating and work harder no matter the cost.

At the end of the semester, I turned in a final report in a class that I currently held a ninety-eight grade average. I was asked by my teacher to see her because she thought I had plagiarized my paper. I went to her office and told her the exact truth of where I got my information for my paper and which references I had used. To make a very long, detailed story short, I was dismissed from the graduate program for plagiarism.

And if you're wondering, I'll be completely honest with you. I didn't even intentionally plagiarize my paper. I didn't include all of my references at the end of my paper, but I didn't try to hide anything when I was confronted about it. It was an honest mishap on my end.

I had finally got my act together.

Finally started working harder.

I had been praying to God to forgive me for cheating and help me do honest work and this was his answer? Dismissal from a graduate-level program?

I was a bit frustrated with God at this point. I didn't understand, and quite frankly I didn't want to. Sometimes in life just when you think your faith is at an all-time high, something happens that makes you question it all over again. However, I continued to pray for His will to be done in all of this. I trusted that He had a plan far bigger than what I had expected, even if I didn't agree with the path.

I took a break from school and started working for UPS, loading trucks in the early morning hours. Working there fueled my desire even more to go back to graduate school. With the help of my wonderful wife (fiancée at the time), I learned of an OT school in Memphis, Tennessee. I prayed to God faithfully and then decided to take off to Memphis, leaving behind my fiancée, family, and friends.

With only one day left until I packed up and left Arkansas, I still had no place to stay once I got to Memphis. Furthermore, if it wasn't for the help of my parents, I wouldn't have had much money. The good news was that my prayer life had changed and my faith had grown, and thank goodness because I was about to be homeless in a place where I knew no one.

Little did I know that as I was heading to pick up the moving truck and load up my stuff, another prayer was being answered. I received an e-mail from a minister in Memphis who said that someone from the church had a place for me to stay. I found out all of this within twenty-four hours before leaving to Memphis!

Even with a prayer being answered of having a place to stay, I knew that I was moving to a new place without even knowing if I would be accepted into the graduate program there.

Also, before I left for Memphis, I wanted to make sure that I had work lined up before moving there to pay for rent, bills, and other essentials. I had applied for a job through the Internet and received a phone interview for the open position about two weeks before leaving for Memphis.

On the third or fourth day, I was in Memphis, I had a face-to-face interview in which the interviewer told me I had the job. Two days after being told I had the position, I got a call from the lady who had interviewed me. She told me that she wasn't going to be able to offer me the job after all due to unforeseen circumstances. I remember hanging up the phone and standing on the back deck of the mobile home I was staying in and just staring off into space for several minutes.

Once again I was frustrated with God, and I didn't understand what He wanted me to do.

I was praying faithfully and trusting Him, but I was in Memphis now with no family, no friends, and away from my fiancée. And to top it all off, I had very little money and no job.

I guess it stands to reason why praying faithfully is so hard. We live in a "drive-thru" society, and we want things our way and we want them now! We want our order quickly and exactly the way we ask for it! We certainly don't have time to wait on God!

However, when we pray, God works in His time. Not in ours. That's what makes praying so difficult. We want instant results to our gratification. If that's where you're at in your prayer life, you might need to reevaluate why you pray in the first place.

A few days after receiving the news of no job, I got plugged into a local church where I knew I would find peace, comfort, and spiritual support. Eventually, after a couple of months and some patience, I was able to find a job. Six months later, I got married and my wife moved to Memphis. A few months after that, I got a letter stating that I was accepted into OT school!

While in graduate school, I kept a strong prayer life in order to stay focused on my studies because I knew there would still be temptations to cheat. I made sure to put a lot more effort into graduate school this time around, so I made a *conscious* effort to be fully involved in the graduate program. I became the community volunteer coordinator for my class, organized a golf tournament and other fundraising events to fly our class out to San Diego for our annual conference, and joined the work-study program.

After almost three years in Memphis, I was blessed to graduate from OT school and return to Arkansas where I accepted a job at a local hospital.

Now, I didn't tell you all of this to brag about how my prayer life is perfect and how God *always* works out things for *our* good. First of all, my prayer life is not perfect, as I am still learning to pray more faithfully, more intently, more often, and leave it all at His feet. And let me tell you, as you may already know, it's very hard to pray this way.

Second of all, God may not always work things out in your favor or as you envisioned. He is, however, working things out for *His purpose* because at the end of the day, we are created in *His image* for *His glory*.

Thirdly, I wanted to share this with you not only to discuss the power and importance of prayer, but also to encourage you to never give up on your dreams and your goals. People will hurt you, make fun of you, bring you down, and then stomp on you when you get there. However, you have the ability to get back up, dust yourself off, and stay focused on what's important. Don't get even. Get living. Remember this: Just because someone tells you that you can't do something, it doesn't mean you have to listen.

Sometimes life throws you curveballs, but you can sit back, have some patience, and make contact. People will give up on you, and you may even want to give up on yourself. God never does though. And I don't just say that because that's what a Christian is supposed to say. I've been through some difficult times, and I've seen Him do glorious things in my life.

Back to prayer. As I mentioned before, I wanted what's best for me.

"God, I pray that you make me happy and comfortable."

That was my prayer, and whether I actually said those words or not, it's how I felt. As you start your OFY journey, make prayer a vital part of your life. But pray that God opens doors for you and when He does, you will enter without hesitation. Tell God that you're all in and going to make every effort to overcome your past and start a fresh, new life. Be prepared and willing to accept His answer because He may "dismiss you from graduate school" to wake you up and change you for the better.

Pray to Whom? Is Anyone There?

If you skipped straight to this page, it might be because you don't believe in prayer or you've prayed before and feel as though God hasn't listened.

First of all, I'm not going to fault you for feeling either way. I'm sure there have been life experiences that led you to think one way or the other. Having faith in praying to someone we can't see makes us very vulnerable and may even seem silly. Being vulnerable may cause us to stumble or lose faith altogether because we put all of our trust "on the line" hoping that God will hear our prayer.

It could be that you may have had someone close to you in your life who was suffering for no apparent reason. Maybe you have suffered for no cause of your own. Maybe you have lost a close friend or family member all of a sudden. Where was God during those times? I can honestly say that I've never lost someone extremely close to me, nor have I felt deep emotional or physical suffering. With that in mind, I'm not going to pretend that I know what you've gone through or are currently going through. All I can say is that God has a plan for everything. I can't explain why certain things happen, but I don't think we're supposed to know the *why of everything*.

If you have experienced suffering or are currently experiencing pain that has caused you to turn away from God and prayer, please find a person who has been through similar difficult times in his or her life and has found strength and a renewed sense of purpose. If you don't know of anyone, please contact OFY through social media or e-mail, and we will connect you a mentor who has experienced such pain, suffering, and loss that can help you so much more than the words in this book.

The Man Who Didn't Believe

My family likes to have yard sales. We have had yard sales every year since I can remember. A few years ago, we had an older gentleman come to our yard sale who lived in the trailer park across the street. He bought a few items including a blow-up mattress. He asked me to come to his home and show him how to set up the mattress.

I said, "Sure," and followed him to his mobile home.

After showing him how to set it up, I decided to talk with him for a moment by asking him about his family, what he did for a living, and so on. As we're talking, he mentioned to me that he had been struggling with his health for quite some time. Life had been hard for him for a while now because he had little to no money on top of his diminishing health. Although I couldn't feel his pain and suffering, I could see it on his face and through his voice. I asked him if I could pray with him right there in his home. He looked at me, and I'll never forget what he said next, "I'm not sure. I don't really do the whole prayer thing."

I didn't think any less of him for that answer. After all, I knew very little of his past and what he had been through, so I followed up his answer with this, "I believe in a God who cares about me and listens to every prayer I offer up. I believe He meets us where we're at and can heal us no matter what we've done before or what we've been through. If you don't mind, I'll just say a quick prayer on your behalf."

With contemplating eyes, he said, "OK."

I put my hand on his shoulder, bowed my head, closed my eyes, and said a prayer for him. I prayed for his health and healing. I prayed for God to give him strength and comfort.

After the prayer, I looked up and noticed he had tears running down his cheeks. Naturally (yes, I say naturally because it's perfectly okay for men to cry and show emotion), I started to cry with him.

With watery eyes, he said, "Thank you."

So why did a prayer for a man who really didn't believe in its power, bring tears to his eyes and fill his heart with gratitude?

I can't give you the exact answer to what he was thinking or feeling that day, but I can offer a couple of thoughts. I believe he had that reaction for two reasons.

One reason being that I took the time to talk with him and learn a little bit about his life. Speaking for Christians, we seem to do a very poor job of meeting people where they're at. We expect them to be on our level, even though they haven't had the same life experiences we've had.

Shame on us.

Better yet, shame on me.

I remember trying to get people to believe what I believed without ever seeking out a relationship with them. Without ever getting to know them. It was like I was superior to them and they were wrong for not being on my level.

It doesn't work that way and for good reason. This was not what Jesus taught and absolutely not the life Jesus led. Jesus did not come to be served, but to be a servant.

If you are not a Christian (or was and left that life) because someone belittled you or made you feel inferior when you made a mistake, I apologize fullheartedly and ask that you forgive me or anyone else who treated you that way. Even though humans are sinful and tend to make huge mistakes from time to time, God doesn't give up on you. I hope you can find a way to reconcile with God and forgive the person or persons who treated you like you weren't worthy because you're most *definitely* worthy.

If you are a Christian and your approach is to belittle and demean those who aren't on "your level," please reconsider your duty as a Christian. Shoving God down people's throats is not found anywhere in scripture. Compassion, forgiveness, and love are, however.

Don't you want people to join you in the same salvation that God has given you? Every person you see is a child of God created in His image. We should want everyone we meet to experience His love and forgiveness. So get to know where people are coming from. Get to know their background. *Get to know people.*

Then, and only then, can we come together as one in Christ. Maybe this is a part of your OFY journey? If so, commit to it with every ounce of compassion and every inch of love in your body.

Back to the original story. The second reason for his reaction was because there is something emotional and powerful in praying to a higher being that created you from dust, *especially when that prayer is shared with someone during his time of struggle.*

It's interesting to note that both George and this man made a huge, positive impact on my life. As I noted earlier, just when you think you are making a difference in someone's life, you'll be pleasantly surprised to realize that he or she is making an even bigger impact on you.

There are many opportunities presented to you in life to share a moment with someone. To share your struggle with someone who is suffering the same. A lot of times we pass on those opportunities never knowing how those moments could have a lasting, positive effect on us and everyone else.

Maybe you don't believe in God. Maybe you think it's all a myth. Whether you think those things are true or not, I believe that prayer brings about a feeling of peace and comfort. Those feelings were felt by that man in the mobile home regardless of his past life or current level of faith.

My wife and dad are school teachers. My dad has been a teacher for about sixteen years. My wife has been a teacher for about four years now. In those twenty years combined, they have had experience working in different school districts with different philosophies on disciplinary measures. Most of the schools they have taught in do not believe in corporal punishment and don't allow prayer. We'll set aside the corporal-punishment argument for another day.

But here is a fact: The schools they have taught in that allow prayer have fewer fights and expulsions. They have higher grades and overall the students are more connected. Is this coincidence or is there a deeper explanation? The simple explanation is that prayer binds people together. If nothing else, it brings a sense of peace to an otherwise disharmonious planet.

Take a moment now and evaluate your prayer life. As with everything else you write down in this book, be honest with yourself.

For those who pray:

Write down how often you pray.

Circle which one(s) that best describes your *current* prayer life:

Routine   Selfishly   Short and Quick

Rarely   Intentional   Humbly

Emergency Only   Open and Honest   Alone

With Family/Friends   Only Before Meals

Should you pray more often?

Looking back at what you circled, do you feel you could pray differently? How so?

For those who don't pray:

Write down why you don't pray.

Circle yes or no if you believe that prayer can provide peace.

Yes   No

Will you give prayer a second (or first) chance during your OFY? Why or why not?

Hopefully, the reflective questions will help you determine the best course of action to your prayer life during your OFY and the rest of your life.

Don't Just Pray

As this chapter closes, I want to briefly touch on something I mentioned at the very beginning.

Prayer is a great thing. I believe in its power and purpose when used faithfully and selflessly. But is it doing any good if we just tell people that we will pray for them, but not actually do it? I have told people that I would "keep them in my prayers" and then forgot about it. Other times I didn't take the time to pray for them. Furthermore, I have also said the same thing to people when, in fact, I could have physically helped them or provided them with a specific need, not just pray. There are several situations in which people need our prayers. In some of those situations, the best and only thing we might be able to do is pray. However, ask yourself if you can do more. Assess the situation and lend your time and a helping hand if possible. More often than not, you have an opportunity to *do more than just pray.*

My challenge to you is to pray for *everyone* whom you say you will pray for, even if that means praying *for* someone or *with* someone immediately upon becoming aware of his or her need. And, instead of *just* praying for people, find a way to reach out and serve them. Give them your time. Show them your compassion. Offer people help, hope, and healing. *Don't just pray.*

Find a Way to Pray

If you've read through this chapter and still don't think you will pray, please find someone who will pray for you.

If you believe in prayer, pray like you mean it. Pray to God that you're all for positive changes no matter what it takes. Pray for wisdom, strength, and guidance to make positive changes for an entire year. Trust in God to help you on your OFY journey and every journey thereafter.

While you might decide that there are some changes during your OFY that may not need specific prayer (watching less TV, taking the stairs, or riding your bike to work to name a few), just remember to pray differently and faithfully.

Pray for *everyone* who you tell, "I will keep you in my prayers."

Find ways to help people who are in need of prayer, instead of *only* praying.

Pray for all those who are on this journey of change.

Pray for your positive changes to impact the world now and for many more years to come.

Authentic Relationships,

Mentorship and Accountability with Compassion,

Breaking Societal Norms,

Success over Failure,

Prioritizing Time, and

Praying Intentionally

equal

The Perfect Team for Positive Change

Chapter 8

Compare Yourself to No One

We like to try and live up to everyone's expectations but our own. We often think to ourselves, "If I could just be more like (fill in the blank), my life would be so much better." And if we're honest with ourselves, we often think that other people are happy because of their possessions, so we try to "keep up with the Joneses." It could be that we get upset because it seems that troubles and tribulations often find us all the time, while others are living in perfect harmony.

Whatever the case may be, you have to realize that your OFY journey is as unique as you are as an individual.

I researched the top ten New Year resolutions. You probably don't even have to guess that the number-one resolution almost every year is to lose weight. So, other than mentioning to you already that commitment is a huge factor in not completing New Year Resolutions, what else is going on here?

Let's think about weight loss for a minute.

There are what seem like billions of different weight-loss solutions. From weight-loss supplements to 682 different ab workouts. From seven-minute workouts to hours spent in a gym. From liquid-only diets to protein diets; there's a bit of everything. This amount of information can be overwhelming, and it becomes difficult to know which idea will work for you. While this amount of information makes it hard to know where to start, I don't even think this is the biggest reason in not completing a weight-loss plan.

I think the biggest problem is the "after" picture.

You know how every company advertising a weight-loss product shows a before and after picture? It's almost always some man or woman with every outline of every muscle showing. Wow, look at those results! But how long *after* the before picture was the after picture taken? What did that person eat while working out? Did he or she have a personal trainer? Did he or she really only wear a belly-burner brace and get those kinds of results? Did he or she get a tummy tuck? Who knows?

The problem is that we desire the "after" picture even though *the before picture is not us.* Our genetics are different; our resources may be few; and we may have to realize that we can't be like the "after" picture no matter what we do. The truth is that if you set a goal for yourself, you will be less likely to give up a month or two later when you're not seeing any "results." If you compare yourself to the way the world wants you to look, you will always come up short. But that's not to say that you shouldn't care about your body and keep it healthy. It's to say that you don't have to live up to society's standards. If weight loss is a part of your OFY journey, don't set your sights on looking like someone else's "after" picture! Set a goal for *yourself* and build on it after you have completed the first year. Make a commitment to continue with your healthy lifestyle.

As I mentioned earlier, a lot of what we do is based on how others perceive us. Our decisions may be based on traditions or from a learned behavior taught by our society. Sometimes we do or say things that we don't even think about at all because it's become the "norm."

Our tongue can be the most lethal weapon we possess. In a matter of seconds, we can open our mouth and say something that can cause deep pain and suffering to the listener and sometimes it can even cause pain to an unintended receiver. Sometimes we say hurtful things because we're prideful people and don't want our "buddies" to think less of us. We believe that we have to say things in front of certain people to get the attention and praise we desire. Other times we are influenced by movies, TV shows, and music that have a negative message and we don't even realize it.

Part of this journey is to choose to be *different* in a *positive* way. You've watched the news.

You know what words and actions cause anger and strife. Instead of exhibiting the same behavior, you have to strive to be the light in a dark world.

As you start to think about the positive changes you want to make, ask yourself why you say and do what you do. In other words, are you saying things that you don't really mean to say because you picked it up through society or tradition? Are you doing things that you know you shouldn't do just because a friend talked you into it or you saw someone doing it on TV? Think about it.

If I Could Be Like That

"We need more room. If we just had a nice house life would be so much easier, and we would be so much happier."

These are words that my wife and I said on two separate occasions. The first time when we lived in a small, much older mobile home in Memphis. It was just us and an occasional house guest by the name of *Mickey*, so it's not like we needed a ton of room, but *we needed more.* The second time those words were said was when we were living in a small apartment after moving back to Arkansas.

About a year after that, we finally got our new house, equipped with three bedrooms, two bathrooms, and a garage! But something was wrong. It didn't make us any happier. I mean, the house itself did not cause our level of happiness to increase. As with most new, expensive items, more bills and more responsibilities come with it.

This is just one example of a thousand more.

"If I just had a new car"

"If I just had a bigger house"

"If I just had a house on the beach"

"If I just had more money"

"If I just had (insert earthly possession here)"

It's an endless cycle that never reaches true happiness. In other words, our gratification is only fulfilled for a short time until we buy something bigger, newer, or more up-to-date. We measure our happiness by what we have, how much money we make, and how well we're keeping up with society's trends and standards. Instead, our happiness should be measured in how much we give, how much we love, and how much we serve others. There's nothing wrong with a nice house or having financial security. But are you using your possessions to serve or to be selfish and ostentatious?

If part of your OFY is to save up money to buy a car or a new house, that's perfectly fine. Those are good goals to have, but don't let those things become the focal point of your life. If you work hard to obtain them, thank God for His blessings, and then use them to bless others. Invite people over for dinner. Use your house as a safe haven for teens instead of the streets. Use your car to give people a ride to work, church, or some other event. The list could go on and on.

It's time for an illustration with your help. Below, you will see the words "True Happiness." Take your pen or pencil, and draw a circle to the left of those words.

TRUE

HAPPINESS

The circle represents our desire and chase for worldly possessions and wealth. Now, take your writing utensil, and trace over the circle you've already drawn five times.

How many times did your circle touch the words True Happiness?

It never will. That's because worldly possessions can only provide us *temporary* happiness before we crave more and then even more after that.

Worldly possessions and wealth can never bring about "True Happiness."

I'll be honest with you. When I completed my first OFY, I had a feeling of euphoria. The fact that I could make positive changes for an entire year gave me an immense amount of joy, which shifted my focus toward serving others. I also gained a renewed feeling of self-worth and happiness. This feeling was anything but temporary and continued to stay with me as I started my second journey. The happiness I felt was real, long-lasting, and *true*. For that reason, your OFY will bring about a feeling of "treuphoria."

So what exactly is treuphoria?

Treuphoria: An intense feeling of excitement and true happiness that is obtained when you make it through your OFY of positive changes. This feeling is also obtained through selflessness, serving others, and showing compassion.

Treuphoria is a mind-set that we can create that gives us a feeling of contentment no matter what we possess. It's found in our selflessness, devotion, and compassion shown to everyone else. It's found within your OFY journey to make positive changes, to motivate other people to be better, and to uplift and encourage others in their time of sorrow and suffering. The joy you experience in doing those things surpasses any desire to have more possessions or to be like someone else.

When I was twelve years old, the Nintendo 64 was the hottest gaming console on the market. That's right. A sixty-four-bit processing unit was the best console around. I remember telling my parents, "If you get me an N64 for Christmas, I'll never ask for anything ever again!" Being the loving parents that they are, they bought me one. And being the honest son that I am, I kept my promise and never asked for anything ever again.

Just kidding.

Of course I asked for a ton of stuff after that. Why? Because the N64 only provided temporary happiness. There was so much more cool stuff that came out through the years that made the N64 seem obsolete. (For those of you reading this and think that the N64 is the best console ever created, I won't argue with you.) Even at a young age, we realize that the pursuit of "things" never satisfies our desire to be fulfilled, happy, and content.

Society tries to sell you happiness. There are images and ideas that are planted in your brain of what you are to do and possess to be happy. We see pictures of people in large houses, expensive cars, and fancy clothing with big smiles on their faces. Are they truly happy? Do you think to yourself, "If I could be like that person, life would be good"? I've been there before, but I finally realized that God created me and you differently for a reason. His purpose for us should outweigh our desire to possess earthly goods that can vanish quicker than it takes for us to obtain them.

He gave us different talents and abilities so we could make an exclusive, unique impact on the world. Those talents may not be public speaking or something similar that people notice. Those talents might be donating time and money to people in great despair or visiting sick children in a local hospital. God sees all you do and rewards you in due time.

Maybe you're not exactly sure what your talents are yet, but I can guarantee you this: you are a uniquely gifted person with an incredible ability to make positive changes and make the world a better place.

So compare yourself to no one because there is no one quite like you.

Chapter 9

Find It within Yourself

Did I mention yet that you are a wonderful and unique individual? And that you have an incredible ability to make the world a better place?

And trust me, you can.

For years, you may have let fear, disappointment, or discouragement keep you from growing in your faith and overall well-being. Don't let those things defeat you this time. I have been fortunate enough and blessed to be able to graduate college and start my career, but completing my OFY journey was among the hardest and greatest accomplishments I have ever achieved. My second OFY journey, which I am currently on at the time of writing this, is even more exciting than the first.

Throughout your journey, there will be different stages of difficulty. At certain times during your full year, you may experience withdrawal, tiredness, and exhaustion. You may find your journey not even worth completing. In the next few pages, I have listed four phases that you might experience during your journey and some ideas on how to get through each phase on your way to completing your OFY.

The Climb

As you get to the second to fourth months, you might start to realize that it's a long way up the mountain, and the drive to stay on your journey may start to diminish.

This period of your journey is called "The Climb." The Climb is the hardest phase to get through. During this phase, you may have several "voices" telling you to go back to your old ways. You may tell yourself that your bad habits and everyday routines were much easier before, even if you weren't happy. You may even have the urge to quit because you have already failed in the first few months.

While these ideas on the surface seem to be the easier choice, *do not give in and do not give up!*

You made a commitment, remember?

We are building a community of change so hopefully, you will have a close friend or family member to help you on your journey. Maybe both of you are on the journey together. Find a mentor who has been through the same challenges and has found ways to commit and accomplish. By wearing the One Full Year bracelet, you might even find a "stranger" who is committing to the same changes as you and develop a friendship that lasts a lifetime. If you don't have anyone to turn to, please visit the One Full Year website and contact me or an OFY advocate who can encourage you and give you some pointers to help see you through your journey.

Use every good resource available to you. Don't feel lonely because you're not. So many other people have been through the same struggles and changes. There are many others who are currently on their OFY journey as well! Think of it as being on a worldwide team for positive change!

Take one day at a time and fight through. Don't worry about what's behind you or what lies ahead of you. Control the *now*!

The Pinnacle

This phase will likely occur during the fifth to seventh months. You have made it through "The Climb" and you are now at "The Pinnacle" of the mountain! Some people, if not everyone, might say that getting to the top of the mountain is a much better feeling than coming back down. You've journeyed through the rough and steep terrain and now you get to take in the beautiful surroundings! This is certainly true of getting to this point in your OFY journey. Making it this far is quite an accomplishment! Take a moment to realize how strong and committed you are!

Despite the joy of reaching the Pinnacle, there are two things about this phase that make it difficult. First of all, you still have to make it back down the mountain. Second, depending on what you're changing, you might start to realize that no one is there to acknowledge your changes.

While it's very likely that people have noticed or are starting to notice your changes, no one is giving you any praise. It might even be that some of the people closest to you are still continuing their negative behaviors and it's impacting your progress and starting to frustrate you.

This is what makes getting past this phase difficult—continuing your journey when no one is giving you credit for your changes.

You might even ask yourself, "How do I continue to work hard on making positive changes if someone close to me can't forgive my past or constantly brings up my bad habits that I'm trying to overcome?"

To put the answers simply, reread chapter 6. Remember, you cannot control people's words or actions toward you, but you can control yourself. Keep working on your positive changes, and even though a close friend or spouse may say hurtful things, your strong will and determination may provide just the right amount of inspiration to help them discover that they too can make positive changes in their life.

I understand it's a lot easier to feel good about your accomplishments when other people acknowledge them. For example, when you graduated from high school or college, people gathered together to support you and others walk across a large stage to receive your diploma. If you've played sports on any level, you have had fans cheer you on during the game. Don't expect this. Don't expect someone to compliment you even if he or she does notice your positive changes. Don't expect pats on the back or any type of positive reinforcement for that matter.

Even if you have been receiving praise and positive encouragement until this point, keep your thoughts and focus on your goals. Something or someone could sneak up on you and influence you to take a break and eventually steer you off your path.

Keep in mind that you are making these changes to better yourself, and ultimately and more importantly, better others. Furthermore, if some of your changes are very personal and only contained in your letter, people may not know what changes you're even making.

Once again, if you need encouragement and inspiration, get a mentor or an accountability partner. I can't stress this point enough during the first two phases. If you start to waver and struggle, it is very important that you find someone to lift you up. If you don't ask for guidance or support, you may never make it past the Pinnacle phase. I promise that if you can make it to the seventh month, you can make it through the entire year.

You are *over* halfway there. Be determined. Continue to throw every positive and uplifting resource in your direction.

The Tumble

This phase reminds me of a time when I was about twelve years old and went hiking on a mountain near Blanchard Springs in northern Arkansas. As I was walking down the mountain, I saw the end of the trail up ahead. I decided that I wanted to be the first one there and started to run past my cousins who were ahead of me. I didn't pay much attention to my path or the surroundings as I aimlessly ran down the mountain. I soon found out that rocks plus uneven terrain plus running equaled disaster. Before I knew it, I was tumbling down several feet of mountainous ground. Luckily for me, when I reached the end, I had only scraped some of the skin off my right knee to which the scar today is now almost completely gone. No broken bones. No head injury. Just a bloody knee.

During "The Tumble" phase you may see the finish line in sight and start to run aimlessly and recklessly toward the end. First of all, don't live through each day forgetting about the road you have chosen. Second, keep your mind focused on your path and where it is leading you.

When I went through this phase, I started to "tumble" off my path. I could see the end in sight, but I wanted to veer off the path as much as possible without actually getting lost. I remember specifically taking a week or two off during this phase. I didn't fail or give up during this time, but I pushed my OFY out of my mind temporarily. I wanted a "break" from thinking about it. It wasn't until the end of that second week that I realized I hadn't thought much about it. I immediately kicked my journey back into full gear, and honestly became more excited about it than when I first started.

In this phase, which is around the eighth to tenth month, redirect and refocus your thoughts on where you were in the beginning. In other words, go back to the very first week of your journey and think about how excited and enthusiastic you were about starting. Now, apply that same mind-set to where you're at now. Don't aimlessly "tumble" down the remaining path of your journey. Read through this book again and remember the things you jotted down. Renew your purpose and mission.

The Base Line

This phase is the last couple of months before your journey ends. It's a very exciting time to know that you have made it this far. You're probably starting to think you're finished, but don't get ahead of yourself. While you may be able to see how your changes are making a huge impact on you and others, keep in mind that you have a month or two to go.

During this phase, it can be very easy to sit back and relax until your OFY date arrives. Maybe you want to get through with as little effort as possible. You might start to think that ten months was long enough, but don't get too comfortable.

For just a moment, let's step away from the mountain theme and let's examine a race.

If you have ever watched an Olympic long distance runner, you will notice that even after running several miles they still manage to sprint and push themselves as hard as they can for the last two hundred meters.

Why do they do this? Maybe a better question is this: How is it even possible to go *that* fast after running *that* long?

The answer is simple—sheer determination and willpower. The runners know how close he or she is to the finish line. They can see the destination, and those athletes want nothing more than to make that final stride and cross the line. When they see the finish line, they run with a purpose. They have trained and disciplined their bodies for several years to do one thing, finish the race. As they cross the finish line, they propel their bodies forward and throw their arms up in the air as they take their first foot across the line. That feeling of crossing the line is the best feeling in the world. It's a feeling of hard work, discipline, and determination. It's a "man, that feels good" moment!

I named this phase the "Base Line" because as you approach the base of the mountain and you cross the finish line of the race, do so with purpose. Finish strong and finish with arms lifted up!

Once your *first* OFY comes to an end, celebrate your accomplishments, and reminisce on everything you went through to get to this point in your life.

Remember once again that even though you have completed your first OFY of positive changes, there are thousands of other opportunities for you to build on your changes and find new things to change in the years to come!

Next, share your awesome journey with others. Encourage someone to start his or her own journey and give advice on how to see it through. Uplift and inspire people.

Finally, take those accomplishments and start training for the next year because in order to live a happier and healthier life and make the world a better place...

We've got a lot of mountains to climb. And those mountains aren't going to climb themselves.

The Start to a New Beginning

As your reading comes to a close and you start a new journey in life, I want you to remember a few important things:

1. Everything you read in the previous chapters is meant to challenge, motivate, and encourage you to make positive changes and be a better, happier person. To give you hope and inspire you to keep going. These words are not "steps" or "how-tos." They are challenging thoughts to make you think and help you find your own treuphoria. Remember, the drive to change lies within you. Shift into gear and don't let off the pedal.

2. This journey is ultimately about building relationships and community. When you commit to your OFY journey, you are becoming a part of a special group of people who are all on different journeys with the same destination: A Better Life.

3. Share your journey and then share your results. Remember, while there are some things that you will only share with your TALC, there may be

some positive changes that you are working on that you would like to share with others. With your passion and drive, you can inspire and encourage others to begin their own OFY journey. After completing your journey, share your accomplishments and results. Have a sit-down to discuss and talk with your TALC about your full year.

4. *Do not force people to change.* Maybe you know someone who needs to make changes in his or her life. Lead by example, show compassion, and encourage, but remember that it's ultimately up to that person to make changes. *They* have to be willing to commit. Hopefully, by your kind words and actions, they will be inspired to make that commitment.

5. This is only the beginning. Celebrate your accomplishments exactly one year from your start date, but remember that this is *not* the end. The goal is to build upon your first journey and create many full years. There are *always* things we can change and do better.

6. You may or may not have noticed that I repeated a lot of the same thoughts throughout this book. Thoughts such as "make positive changes to

better yourself and ultimately make the world a better place," or "commit to your journey for an entire year," or "conscious effort." I purposely did this to ingrain these thoughts and ideas in your mind. If you want to truly change the world, you must first change yourself. And if you want to truly change yourself, you must first change your attitude, your outlook, and your mind-set.

7. No matter what society tells you. No matter what hatred and negativity is in the media. No matter how many times someone told you that you couldn't do something. No matter what mistakes you've made in your past or how many times you failed before. This is your moment to change for the better and change for a lifetime. So be convinced of what you can accomplish!

Chapter 10

Your Chapter Begins

This is your chapter. In the next few pages, you can write down the positive changes you are going to make. Use the pages to write out your changes and journal your progress every three to four months. If you're not ready today to make those changes, that's okay...to an extent. You have to be willing to fully commit for an entire year, so once you're all in, you are all in! But, if you're having doubts, don't let those second thoughts win this time.

Remember, don't make excuses, and start finding answers. Once more, find someone you can trust to help you on your journey. If you don't have that someone, or don't feel comfortable to talk about the things you need to change, you can always visit the OFY website or find OFY on social media to receive uplifting and encouraging information to keep you motivated on your journey.

You are Capable.

You are Worthy.

Because You Can.

Good luck and get ready to enjoy a renewed life full of positive changes and true happiness!

I hope you're excited about your personal OFY journey after reading the previous chapters. Take a moment right now and pray about the things you know you need to change. Don't want to pray? Call or text someone immediately who you know will pray for or with you. Still don't have anyone to pray for you? Contact OFY through social media or our website, and I promise that we will not only pray for you, we will help you in any way possible throughout your journey!

My thoughts to a better me:

Which will lead to a better world:

To Be Continued...

Vvvvvvvvvvv gy7o90

When my son was first able to walk, he came up to me at the kitchen table and reached out his arms for me to hold him. I quickly lifted him up and sat him in my lap. As soon as he could, he reached up to my keyboard and typed the above letters right in the middle of my paragraph. My first reaction was to show anger and put him down, but I calmly and lovingly directed his attention to something else at the table.

I kept these characters at the bottom of this book throughout the entire duration of my writing as a reminder that there are many things to get upset and angry about throughout our life, but if we just take a moment before we react, we may realize that it's really not worth getting worked up over.

The next time something triggers you to have a negative, impulsive reaction, remember the above letters: twelve v's, space, gy7o90, then smile and know that it's not as bad as you first thought it was.

Thank you for reading and believing in positive change. Blessings to you and all the people you have a positive impact on in the years to come.

Notes

1. A. Lenhart, "Teens, Social Media & Technology Overview," April 8, 2015, accessed April 24, 2017, http://www.pewinternet.org/2015/04/09/teens-social-media-technology-2015/.

2. J. B. Stewart, "Facebook has 50 minutes of your time each day. It wants more," *New York Times*, May 5,2016, https://www.nytimes.com/2016/05/06/business/facebook-bends-the-rules-of-audience-engagement-to-its-advantage.html.

3. *Merriam-Webster*, s.v. "prayer, accessed May 14, 2017, https://www.merriam-webster.com/dictionary/prayer.

Please visit the OFY website for more information on how to create long-lasting positive changes within yourself and your community. You can find gear, books, mentors/advocates, and other uplifting resources on the OFY website at onefullyear.com

Get your "Gear for the Year" to keep your mind focused on pursuing positive changes for an entire year and beyond. The Gear will also open up conversations and help spread positive change throughout the world!

A portion of every purchase from the website will go toward funding and supporting positive changes that are already being made in the community, creating and establishing programs to inspire positive change where we see a need, and globalizing the message of positive change and a renewed commitment to Christ.

Connect with us on Facebook, Instagram, and Twitter. The more you like and the more you share, the more we can inspire positive change throughout the world.

Send all your letters and uplifting messages to

One Full Year
PO Box 7093
Sherwood, AR 72124